In vitro veritas

—

more tracts for our times

St Mary's Annual for 1984/5
edited by Tom Sutcliffe and Peter Moore

St Mary's Bourne Street

The substance of the ancient deposit of faith is one thing, and the way in which it is presented is another — John XXIII.

First published 1984
St Mary's, Bourne Street
St Mary's Presbytery
30 Bourne Street
London SW1W 8JJ

British Library Cataloguing in Publication Data

In vitro veritas: more tracts for our times.
1. Sociology, Christian
I. Sutcliffe, Tom and Moore, Peter
261 BV625

ISBN 0-9508516-1-2

Photoset in Baskerville and Bembo by Ebony Typesetting, Liskeard
and printed in Great Britain by Billing & Sons Limited
Book Plan, Hylton Road, Worcester

Contents

Foreword

John Gilling

St Mary's, Bourne Street has a long tradition of publishing. In the 1920s the clergy of the church were closely associated with the Society of St Peter and St Paul, which, under the patronage of such eminent laymen as Lord Halifax, the Duke of Argyll and other grandees, described itself modestly as 'publishers to the Church of England' and produced tracts and sermons as well as the *Anglican Missal*. So *In vitro veritas: More Tracts for Our Times*, a second volume of Tracts in the 1980s, is no innovation.

Tracts for Our Times, again following our tradition of a critical and open minded catholic conservatism, was a distinct success. It was reviewed not only in ecclesiastical journals but extensively in the secular press with the result that it was all too soon sold out. I hope that the readers of this slim volume, its successor, will not be disappointed: it is good value and good reading.

It is still true, as it was in the 1920s, that the majority of works published about ecclesiastical and theological issues are propaganda either for modernism (if that word is not entirely out of date) or conservative evangelicalism, as are many of the more thoughtful programmes on radio and television. So it is still very much worthwhile to seek to say something rational in favour of traditional doctrines and practices within the Church of England, even if we can hardly hope to amend the balance to any great extent. A number of the essays in this book were commissioned by the Dean of St Albans for a project of his own, along precisely such lines, and we are happy to be able to help bring them before the public.

There is now some evidence that theological liberalism may have at last provoked among the ordinary faithful laity of the church a sense of loss, even of outrage. It is particularly unfortunate that the leading exponents of radicalism, at least as far as the media are concerned, have been bishops and clergymen. Anti-clericalism has never in the last century of the history of our country been much of an issue. But the signs are that it is now beginning to arrive on the scene. It is one of the good things in *Tracts* that the articles are not monopolised by the clergy. I believe that the church in England today needs more lay theologians (like those of the previous generation, C.S. Lewis and Charles Williams) who unite a deeply held loyalty to the universal Christian tradition with an exploratory, questing intellect. It is not the duty of the clergy to repress and bully the laity or to teach them their business, but to encourage their growth in the knowledge and love of God, especially considering that the laity of the church in its innumerable councils — stretching from PCCs to the General Synod — is constantly being asked to deliberate and decide on matters of doctrine and liturgy.

There is no shortage of new books on religious subjects let alone the enormous flood of reports and pamphlets that cover the desks of the clergy, issuing from the central authorities of the church and various pressure groups. To add to their number may seem just to add one more opportunity for mental and spiritual indigestion. But I trust this neat, new book will provoke thought and discussion. And for some of us certainly the controversial nature and tone of much of the writing will come as a shock.

A great cook once said that a good meal should 'astonish the stomach.' I suspect that in these pages there are some articles which we will find it impossible inwardly to digest. Too much pepper? Perhaps. But at least no one can mistake it for gruel or lightly boiled eggs. It would certainly be far too strong meat for a Mr Woodhouse, but today the British have taken to the strong flavours and pungent aroma of exotic cooking. Even if the diet does not wholly agree with us, we may yet be stimulated and excited by it.

St Mary's Presbytery, October 1984.

1

In vitro veritas

Sara Maitland

> This withdrawal from the corporeal world must doubtless be good, since it is advised by such spiritual people, but my belief is that it should be practised only when the soul is very proficient: until then, it is clear, the Creator must be sought through the creatures. Theresa of Avila, *Life* XXII.

In 1633 the Church, using the instrument of the Inquisition, required Galileo to recant of the heresy of Copernicanism (the belief that the earth was not the fixed centre of the created universe, but moved around both its own axis and the sun). Apparently unwilling to sacrifice pointlessly the rest of his life's work, and presumably also desiring to remain within the charity of the Church, Galileo recanted. Legend recounts that as he did so he muttered *'Eppur si muove'* ('But it still does move').

Time, of course, has vindicated Galileo, but it does not seem to have instructed the Church. Symbolically in 1633 the Church decided to elevate 'Revelation through the Tradition' above another of the traditional sources of knowledge: Revelation through the Creation. If science was going to abandon the geo-centric universe with Man (and I use the word with conscious irony) as the centre of the centre, then the Church would abandon science. Theology — once the queen of sciences — abdicated voluntarily from so wide and sweet a kingdom and set up instead what too often looks like a tiny and paranoid dictatorship.

Since then orthodox theology has frequently found itself in impossible positions because of its mulish refusal to accommodate its theory to match the available data. In the nineteenth century evolutionary discoveries and historical scholarship both threw theological discourse into disarray. Holding out for Genesis I and II and for Matthean primacy, for no apparently better reason than that was what they had thought of first, was not helpful to ordinary Christians who wanted to combat secularist *consequences* or *interpretations* by investigating facts in the light of faith.

So of course we should not be altogether surprised to find ourselves once again in theological difficulties in relation to the new knowledge, the new sciences of the twentieth century. Many of the new disciplines — especially perhaps electro-physics — might be more amenable to a traditional Catholic reading than the nineteenth century mechanistic sciences; but theology does not seem to be able to respond. The official theology of Catholism seems to have turned its back on facts learned through the observation of the created order.

Many of the important epistemological developments of this century have been in the area of human relationships at all levels: from Marx's (and others) macrocosmic analyses, through anthropology and sociology, to Freud's (and others) intrapersonal investigations. Our understanding of human nature has — like it or not — changed. Although there is nothing intrinsic to these expansions of knowledge which diminishes the glory and activity of God, (though it may diminish the glory and importance of Man) theology seems extremely reluctant to change to meet them. At the very simplest level Thomistic theology was based on a natural universe that no-one believes in any more: not just geo-centric, but anthropocentric, individualistic and masculist in a way that now seems preposterous.

For example, Aquinas's imagery of a male God creating humanity within the 'womb' of a female Nature, was based on a biology that taught a) that women were 'deficient' men — a view which the present understanding of XY chromosomes and foetal development disproves; and b) that the whole human being was contained in miniature within the spermatazoum and that the uterus contributed no matter but only a nurturing place for the diminutive but fully formed human. All images of God or ethical codes which are based on this 'information' must be regarded critically.

But — particularly in the area of sexual ethics — this critical self-reflection does not seem to be happening. We have no significant theological teaching on psychology, or anthropology. We have no attempts to incorporate the new 'world view' into the imagery we have of God or relationships. And the terms of the discussion between South American Liberation theologians and the Vatican are a dire warning to those who might want to make use more abstractly of Marxism's historical and sociological analyses.

I believe that a large number of the would-be faithful need an answer to a very fundamental question. What should Galileo have done? Should he, for obedience sake, recognising the authority of the magisterium, have recanted, when he was so certain that 'It did still move'? Or should he, for conscience sake, have allowed himself to be damned? And is there any need to put any human being into so intolerable a dilemma?

What follows here is a list of questions which aspects of the catholic teachings on sexual ethics raise for me. They are not the only, nor even necessarily the most important questions, but they are real questions; ones I have to confront in my daily life.

The official teachings of the Church in this area seem to match neither lived experience nor the available factual data (in as much as these should be separate at all). My information comes from an environment which is post-Freud, post-Einstein, post-Marx, and post-feminism. Ethical theology has not challenged the observations of these disciplines, it has chosen to ignore them. Or rather, to try and ignore them: since theologians do not really live in isolated ivory towers, certain bits of information do sneak in, and this actually makes the situation worse; for in its attempt to maintain untenable positions, ethical doctrine is not only teaching some rather peculiar things, it is itself becoming more and more inconsistent as odd snippets are tacked clumsily on to the old fabric.

It is difficult to know where to start because issues of sexuality have been fragmented, but perhaps it is best to begin with some inquiries into the area of reproduction. This is central because the teachings on sexual ethics basically accept that all sexuality, and in particular women's sexuality, revolves around reproduction. Yet most of the evidence suggests that this is not true.

The biological evidence, for instance, includes the menopause and the absence of the oestral cycle in women who, unlike other mammals, are sexually receptive when not fertile. There is also the existence and function of the clitoris, etc. For sociological evidence about sexuality there are the reports of Masters and Johnson, of Kinsey and of Hite. And then there is the personal witness of imaginative works, of questionnaires and of gossip. Yet still this assumption about sexuality, that it is meaningful only in the context of reproduction, underlies too much Christian thinking. (An example almost touching in its naivety is the argument in Humanae Vitae that contraception is a bad thing because 'it may lead a husband to make excessive and inconsiderate demands on his wife.' The question is not only about whether the best way of preventing this is by laying her open to pregnancy should she succumb, but what about the possibility that *she* might want more sex than *he* does?)

In any case, on fairly flimsy grounds, the Church continues to maintain that the only right and full purpose of coitus is the conception of children within marriage. For this reason contraception is unacceptable and contrary to 'natural law'. However the Rhythm

Method (deftly described by Rosemary Ruether as 'the psychological equivalent of the Chinese Water Torture') is now acceptable. The only logical consistency in this — especially now that the Rhythm Method is allowed to include thermometer-graphs, acidity level testing, and cervical mucus examination — is that 'abuse of the natural law' is permissible so long as it is unreliable, uncomfortable and intrusive into the expression of marital affection.

Obviously if ethical teaching held seriously the view that the only proper use of sexual relations was conceiving children then we should all be using the Rhythm Method in reverse; testing and measuring and guessing so that we *only* committed coital acts during fertile periods. What seems to me to be particularly worrying here, is that *all* methods of contraception — except total abstinence from all heterosexual acts — are based on an improved understanding of the complexity and delicacy of women's reproductive biology; both the biology itself and the intelligence to understand it are part of what God made and saw to be good. To suggest that we can properly put this knowledge to use so long as we do so in the most ineffective and (for the couple) the least joy-enhancing way seems to me an insult to the creation as well as to the intelligence.

Arising from these odd perspectives come some even more peculiar positions. One was revealed recently when a couple sought to get married and were refused by their parish priest on the grounds that he did not believe that the man (a paraplegic) was capable of full sexual intercourse. Although it was indicated that the priest had been less than pastorally tactful, the principle was not challenged. The problems raised by this view of 'real sex' are massive, and if we had not so fragmented our ethical understanding would rebound in many directions. For instance if the only 'real' sexual act is one in which a man inserts his penis into a women's vagina and keeps it there until he reaches orgasm, then homosexual activities are not 'sex', and any objection to them disappears. (Clearly at least in the case of lesbian sexual activity the argument of 'perversion of object' cannot be used to get round that one.)

An even more bizarre example of this muddled thinking was produced in Australia. The Bishop's Conference of Victoria in their argument against *in vitro* fertilisation* said that it was unacceptable to Catholics because it necessarily involved an 'unnatural act' —

*There are indeed arguments about *in vitro* fertilisation that require further thought; all I am saying is that this particular argument is extraordinary.

masturbation. Following Pius XII's 1949 dictum, on the subject of artifical insemination — 'It is superfluous to mention that the active element [in itself an inaccurate, male-based description of spermatazoa] can never be obtained legitimately by means of acts against nature.' The implication of this is peculiar: a couple who know that they are infertile may continue to make love — although the purpose of this is to conceive children — but may not seek IVF, which may give them those children, because that would involve masturbation, which of its nature 'damages the relationship between husband and wife.'

This point was challenged more movingly than I could at a conference involving the parents of an IVF child. The question was asked as to whether it was feasible to have IVF programmes which incorporated 'bodily love' — for instance by recovering the sperm after intercourse. The question was a technical one and addressed to a doctor on the panel, but the child's father intervened:

> 'If I may I would like to answer that myself. They say there is no bodily love, but Jan (his wife) and I have always insisted on having a private room and sperm collection is always an intimate and loving thing between Jan and I. It is done together and it is a very tender thing. We do it with total awareness, which is probably more than the average couple does. To us it is very important that she (their daughter) was conceived with bodily love.

A theology which, in the light of present understanding, defines a sexual act, defines bodily love, only as existing in male-orgasmic penetrative 'full' intercourse; and does so because it sees sexuality as only a 'means to the end' of procreating children, is a theology which is not based in human reality. It is also a theology which opens up a hornet's nest of illogical, immoral and damaging consequences.

The Church's duty, surely, is to call people to adulthood; you cannot tell adults (or children actually) that they must *think* something 'because I say so.' Why? On what grounds? Please explain? are all legitimate questions. Perhaps homosexuality, for instance, *is* a 'sin'. But since it does not appear to be a symptom of mental illness, does not damage social relations, and — on the evidence of thoughtful individuals — does not impair their relationship with God, then there is a new question: what is a sin? And the answers that we are given are frequently insultingly inadequate, and wildly inconsistent.

This inconsistency is seen all over the place. It is not necessarily the case that the teachings of official ethics are wrong; it is that the reasons given are an insult to the thinking Christian. Look at Abortion for example. I, and many other women, have very profound problems with the practice of abortion: it is a decision of despair; a grevious pain for a woman to face the fact that the world is intolerable for her and her child; it is a decision which probably will in the long run create a moral climate which is discriminatory and oppressive in new ways.

But to be anti-abortionist is one thing, to turn to the Church for help and discover the best reason they can offer you is that the foetus has a soul from the moment of conception is quite another. In the light of contemporary knowledge the idea of ensoulment from conception is harder to accept than abortion. Take the development of identical twins for instance: for several days after the merging of the ovum and the sperm, the gamete (the technical word for the foetus at this early stage) divides arithmetically, but is completely unified. All the cells in this gamete are unspecified — they can develop into any specific cell function (tissue, bone, organs etc); you can even remove and destroy some of these cells and the foetus will continue to develop normally. This we are taught is a complete and unique human being, possessing a complete and unique soul a beloved child of God. (Interestingly, if it is to die at this point it may not be buried, nor can Requiems be said for it???).

Then this gamete splits and two embryos develop. What, theologically, is held to have happened? Did the soul split in two? Impossible, the soul is indivisible. Did a new soul appear? Impossible, the child had a soul from the moment of conception. Is one of the twins souless? Impossible, obviously. We need (and need quickly before some technician starts cloning from gamete cells, or freezing a few cells for future growth) a whole new way of talking about and imaging human uniqueness; we do not need, and indeed cannot accept, a theology of 'ensoulment' which denies the actual, demonstrable phenomenon of nature. The heights of absurdity were reached in this area by a Bishop who argued recently that it was the duty of Christians to 'people heaven'. Cyncially one must conclude from that — given the ensoulment of the foetus — that it is the duty of every fertile woman to get pregnant and abort as often as possible: you could if you worked on it add at least four souls a year to the heavenly population. I am not being entirely frivolous.

Similarly, in the light of lived experience, how can anyone describe the un-born child as 'innocent' given the teachings of the Church in other areas about the sanctity of human life. If we understand anything of Original Sin, we must in the light of sociological and anthropological insights, understand something of incorporation, of social membership and structure. Just as it is permissible to kill another individual (say a conscripted soldier, or a lunatic) who, though personally guiltless, is endangering either individual or societal life; so it should be possible to admit that for many women a baby is not innocent — 'devoid of harm'. A child may actually and directly threaten a woman's health, well being, material and social environment, sanity, certain avocations (freedoms), to say nothing of life, liberty and the pursuit of happiness. In some women's lives a child is exactly as innocent as a shoal of hungry piranah fish. Ethically we must take a line which either unites an anti-abortionist stance with a complete pacifism or we must permit relativist situationalist concerns to inform our conduct within the whole 'value of human life' discussion.

I could go on and on with these muddled groupings. Confronted with a good deal of the sexual ethics of official teachings my mind is befogged by what seems to be happening. I go back to my original question. I want someone to explain to me what I am supposed to do and feel when I seek to inform my conscience and bend my mind to the mind of the Church and I come across rationales which are irrational; premises about 'nature' which seem to have no support from the 'natural order'; prejudices which do not seem to know that this is what they are; and assumptions (about, just for instance, women) which lead directly to injustice, and by very short paths to idiocy.

Just as Galileo was certain, based on observation and experience and wide reading, that the earth did not move around the sun and that the Church was therefore simply wrong; so am I certain that the nature and meaning of human sexuality in its many and complex manifestations has been misdescribed by official Christian ethics and that this misconception leads to personal pain and social injustice which are both contrary to the will of God.

I believe that this misdescription arises from two associated causes. The first is a failure in the structuring of ethical theology to find a way of incorporating experience. Interestingly this is not so in all areas of theology: the process of canonisation for example requires evidence of a popular cult *before* the investigation from the top can begin. Sexual ethics deny the validity of experience. The second is like unto it: corporeal experience, seeking the creator in the creation, has been denied in favour of the abstracted arguments of philosophies worked out precisely by those least likely to have to confront the actual experience (middle-class, white men — frequently celibate.)

In the last fifty years new and detailed observations have demonstrated not that Newtonian physics was wrong, but that it was inadequate to describe all phenomena. The New Physics has learned that the position and the relative movement of the observer affects what is observed. Perhaps it is time that theology took heed of the moral of the

Galileo story and realised that the premises on which much of its theorising is based are no longer adequate to describe experience. Abstraction has not been God's way; in the Creation and Incarnation God precisely entered into lived — that is to say time-affected — experience. Perhaps the Church could take the same risks with the Tradition as God chose to take in those two ultimately significant acts.

Sara Maitland is a novelist and writer, married to the vicar of St. Chad's, Haggerston, London.

2

And to God the things that are God's

Eric Mascall

'If you had told any typical Christian thinker in any century from the twelfth to the sixteenth that religion had nothing to do with economics, and that bishops must not intrude in these matters upon the deliberations of laymen — propositions which to many of the correspondents to our newspapers appear to be axiomatic — he would either have trembled for your faith or feared for your reason. He would have regarded you, in short, as either a heretic or a lunatic.'[1]

Those words were written by Maurice B. Reckitt in 1934 but they are none the less relevant today. From time to time those who have been made anxious by Dr Edward Norman's protest in his Reith Lectures of 1978[2] about what he describes as 'the politicisation of religion' will quote our Lord's exhortation 'Render to Caesar the things that are Caesar's and to God the things that are God's'[3] as implying a division of human concerns into a 'spiritual' or 'religious' area, which belongs to God, and a 'material' or 'secular' area, which belongs to man and with which God has nothing to do.

In fact our Lord's words imply the precise opposite. When, looking at the image of Caesar on the coinage, he tells them to render to Caesar the things that are Caesar's, no doubt the immediate reaction of his hearers is that which I have described. 'Splendid,' they reflect. 'No need to be bothered by troublesome moral restrictions in matters of business and public life!' But immediately this comfortable attitude is blown sky-high by the rest of the sentence: '— and to God the things that are God's.' For they knew, if many modern economists and financiers do not, that even the things which are Caesar's by a temporary and delegated ownership, are primarily and absolutely the possessions of God, who is their creator and preserver.

---

1. *Religion and Social Purpose* (SPCK 1935), p. 12.
2. *Christianity and the World Order* (Oxford University Press).
3. Matthew xxii, 21, and parallels.

There are religious — Buddhism and some types of Hinduism are examples — which look upon matter and the whole physical component of human existence as either unreal or evil, and for which the religious man or woman is one who lives as far as possible as if he was a purely mental or spiritual being and as if his body and material things were totally irrelevant. (Christians themselves have been often tempted to fall into this error, but it is plainly contrary to the Christian faith.) It has the paradoxical consequence that it allows the whole secular order — politics, economics, education, leisure and so on — to become entirely independent and autonomous, to expand and burgeon without any kind of external restraint, and finally to turn inward upon itself and become self-devouring and suicidal, the fate of which our own civilisation seems to be within measurable distance. And the Lord's words come with stark and uncompromising simplicity to remind us that even what may seem to be the least 'religious' aspects of human activity — those that are focussed in, and symbolised by, Ceasar's image on the coinage — do in fact belong to God and therefore cannot claim exemption from his judgement.

Let us ask, then, in the light of this overarching truth of the universal sovereignty of God, what should be the attitude of a Christian to politics. And first it must be made clear that 'politics' means something much more than 'Should I vote Conservative, Labour or Alliance in the General Election?' but 'What is my concern for the *polis*, the community, the whole social order, of which, whether I like it or not, I am part?' And, while the Christian's faith will not hand him on a plate a simple answer to every conceivable question with which he may be confronted, it will give him a special outlook and insight, simply because he has (or will have, if he has understood his religion at all) a particular belief about the nature, condition and resources of the human beings of whom the community is composed.

We might take as a starting-pint the admirable statement which is placed before its members by the School of Nursing of the University of St Thomas, of Houston, Texas, in the United States; it would be equally relevant to anybody entering upon a course of study anywhere or, indeed, proposing to live anywhere as a human being among human beings:

> We believe that man is a composite being of body and soul created by God for a supernatural destiny, that he possesses intellect and will and is responsible for his conduct; that he is a social being of intrinsic worth and dignity; and that he has both individual and social needs, rights and responsibilities.

This is, of course, only a partial statement of Christian belief; it says nothing about sin or redemption, nothing about the Incarnation or the Resurrection, nothing about the Church and the Sacraments. I shall return to this in a moment. But now I want to stress the importance of the basic Christian assertions about man's nature, destiny and powers; for the weakness of Christian witness is largely due to the fact that most Christians begin their Christian thinking much too far on, with their belief in the Incarnation and the Church, and never consciously reflect that they are also committed to certain very distinctive beliefs, which are dismissed by most of their neighbours as doubtful or even ridiculous, about the basic orientation and needs of human beings as such.

If this assertion seems questionable, I would simply appeal to the experience of taking part, in a mixed gathering of Christians and non-Christians, in a discussion of any current political or social issue and then asking oneself whether the Christians used any other criteria than the non-Christians for the judgements which they expressed. Only too often we see that Christians, instead of making the Christian beliefs about man part of their mental equipment, so that their judgements about social and political issues are made almost instinctively in accordance with them, adopt some political stance on purely secular grounds, generally in accordance with the social class to which they belong, and then, if they are challenged, produce some specious and partial argument to prove that it is really the Christian position. Think, for example, of the way in which it is argued first that democracy is a truly Christian principle and then, in turn, that Conservatism, Socialism and Liberalism are each truly democratic.

I have stressed the necessity of beginning our Christian thinking further back than what are usually thought of as the specifically Christian doctrines, of thinking not only about the Christian doctrines of Christ and the Church, but about the Christian doctrine of man. We must, however, recognise that the Christian doctrine of man in its concrete actuality owed an enormous debt to the doctrines of God and Christ. The notion of a human being as a *person,* with a permanent individuality, with an eternal destiny and an indestructible value, and not just a bubble on the evolutionary process, which contrasts Christianity so strongly with religions such as Hinduism and Buddhism, is an almost direct outcome of the belief that God himself is a Trinity of Persons and that the second Person has quite literally become human.

The tradition of Christian social thinking in Anglicanism, which, beginning with F. D. Maurice, continued through such great figures as

Henry Scott Holland, Charles Gore and William Temple down to our own times, laid its main stress upon the Incarnation as the means by which the Fatherhood of God is shown to be not just an abstract theological concept but a concrete historical reality. In the words of that remarkable prophetic figure Thomas Hancock,

> There is no certainty that God is the Father unless it be true that he has, and ever has had, a coeternal Son. We might by a figure of speech call him *a* Father, but *the* eternal and absolute Father he cannot be, unless there is one who is not merely *a* son but the eternal and absolute Son.

And again:

> This Person of the Undivided Triune Godhead, through whom we can approach and know the Godhead, is already and completely our own. He who is 'Our God' is ours because he is Man. We have not to persuade him to be humane, for he is human. So far is the Church from hiding his real manhood that it is all her hope for herself and for mankind, all her joy, all her glory, all her strength.[4]

And it must be emphasised that the Incarnation — the becoming-man of God the Son — is not a past event but an abiding and indestructible reality. *From the moment when he became man in the womb of Mary the Virgin, God the Son has been a human being, and he is one now.* In the words of one of the recent editors of St Thomas Aquinas, 'the central point of Christian belief is that the maker of the universe is now a man.'[5] It is a sheer mistake to suppose that the Ascension meant that the Incarnation was over, that Jesus, having done his job, was leaving this world and going back to the heaven from which he had come. The precise opposite is the case: the Ascension was the final liberation of Jesus's human nature from the restraints of space and time, so that henceforth he could, through the descent of the Holy Spirit, be present in that human nature in all times and places.

It is his failure to understand this that, for example, led Dr Edward Norman, in his Reith Lectures, to describe the Incarnation by the extraordinary phrase 'the visible and the unseen world were *briefly* joined'[6]. The consequence is that any effective concern of the Christian religion with the world is seen by him as entirely a matter of the past, there are no Christian criteria for judging matters in the social and political realm, and, while a great deal of Christian leadership is rightly

---

4 Quoted from A. M. Allchin, *The Spirit and the Word*, London 1963, p. 55.
5 Kenelm Foster, OP, *Summa Theologiae*, Blackfriars Edition, IX, p. xxi.
6 *Christianity and the World Order,* Oxford 1979, p. 77. (italics mine).

denounced as 'the adoption . . . of the moral and political idealism of the surrounding secular culture,'[7] he has himself capitulated to a cultural conditioning of an unconscious and insidious type. Thus he validly complains that 'China, whose denial of the most basic Human Rights ought to attract the condemnation of those Christians whose liberalism is the most developed, is in practice often treated to positively fulsome praise,'[8] but shows himself as extremely reluctant to admit the evidence of repression by the Soviet government of free expression in Russia, apparently through his unwillingness to admit the concept of human rights at all.

What is, I think, extremely informative for our purpose is the fact that Dr Norman's extreme confusion of thought arises from a basic error in Christian doctrine, which distorts all his subsequent argument. That is his assumption that the Incarnation was a passing episode and is not an abiding reality. Let us see how it affects this question of Human Rights.

Dr Norman has attacked the World Council of Churches and the churches whose social thinking has been affected by it for the excessive emphasis which it has given to the notion of Human Rights, and he has argued that they have derived this not from traditional Christian teaching about the natural moral law but from their politicisation by contemporary liberal secular culture. Now I admit that Christian institutions have sometimes taken refuge in political activism because they have lost their roots in Christian doctrine and feel the need to justify their existence somehow. But I do not think it is often recognised how much any real belief in human rights — I mean belief that there are certain inalienable rights which belong to all human beings regardless of race, colour, intellect and sex — depends upon a theological conviction about the nature of human beings as such and about the relation of God to the human race.

Although the outlook of most people in the technological culture of the First World today may be described as a kind of scientific positivism leaning to atheism, science itself gives no grounds for supposing that human beings are more than highly improbable bubbles on the evolutionary stream with neither permanence nor value. Nor will it be much consolation to be told that for a brief thirty years two millennia ago this world was visited by a transcendent power. If, however, the creator of the universe has himself become a human being, uniting to

7. ibid., p. 32.
8. ibid., p. 12.

himself not one man and woman here and there but the human race in its entirety, in a complete and indissoluble union, then every one of its members, being made to enjoy in Christ nothing less than the life of God himself, is inherently the subject of rights and duties, powers and privileges, that are inalienable and irrevocable. This, if it is properly understood and acted upon, will result not in the politicisation of religion but in the supernaturalisation of politics, that is to say, the taking up, by Christian men and women, of the whole of their political and social life, their membership in the human community, into the offering which they make of their lives to the Lord and Father of mankind as members of his Son, who has taken them up into his own being by becoming one of them. It is this conviction about the present condition and status of the human race in its union with the risen Christ, and not some vague concept of 'democracy' or some academic theory of natural human rights, that must provide both the justification and the content of a Christian social doctrine, though it will be a doctrine by which a natural ethic will be both embraced and transcended.

How closely natural morality is bound up in practice with an acceptance and understanding of man's supernatural dignity and calling is shown by the tragic way in which the cataclysmic abandonment of Christian belief and practice in the First World has gone hand in hand with an accelerating decline in standards of moral behaviour. The increase in violent crime is the most obvious index of the loss of respect for human persons. An even more socially disintegrating manifestation, though it is one which is concealed by highly misleading labels, is in the realm of sexual ethics. The provision of easier and easier divorce as the simplest solution for marital problems not only discourages men and women from discovering and exploring the deep reality of a lifelong marriage union but also inflicts grave deprivation on many of the weakest and most vulnerable members of the community, namely the children; as witness the mounting problem of the 'one-parent families'. And it cannot be too strongly emphasised that divorce, which is always represented as the provision of release from an unjust bondage, is also the refusal of the right of married coupled to have the indissolubility of their union recognised and protected by the state.

But an even more flagrant violation of human rights is the still comparatively recent legalisation of abortion. Though defended by such specious pretexts as 'the right of a woman to dispose of the contents of her own body', an abortion is in fact the deliberate killing of one of the most helpless and innocent members of the human community. The actual way in which human reproduction is arranged is of course in many ways inconvenient and painful, so much so in fact that we are always tempted to devise substitutes or modifications to preserve only its more agreeable features; but reality always has its revenges in the end. I cannot go further into this particular matter here, but on the wider issue it is important to note how easily scientific humanism, when it loses its grip on the Christian doctrine of man as created by God and redeemed by Christ, can slip from extolling man as the supremely valuable species, to whose welfare all others can be rightly subjected, to granting him the lowlier status of a late arrival on the evolutionary scene, whose future is doubtful and possibly quite brief.

It should not be difficult for a Christian to decide on his attitude in any specific social or political issue if he has a live understanding of the Christian belief about man. It is however disturbing to see how often a Christian thinks he can discharge this duty by making a once-for-all commitment to a particular political party, and it is even more disturbing when this party turns out to be the one which offers to people of his own social grade the most substantial material benefits. 'If I am the kind of being that the man who writes the advertisement on the Underground thinks I am, and if I am the kind of being that the man who writes the leaders in my newspaper thinks I am,' William George Peck once remarked, 'then I am not the sort of being the Gospel thinks I am.' How many churchpeople, one wonders, are trained to have that reaction, and to know why they should have it?

In the narrower realm of commerce and finance, the Christian, if he is not himself a commerical and financial expert, may understandably hesitate to intervene, for this is a realm which bristles with technicalities and in which the experts themselves are frequently at odds. Yet there are things that can be and need to be said, and I do not believe that the Christian responsibility is adequately discharged by speeches at city dinners in which financiers and ecclesiastics congratulate each other on the mutually beneficial services which the Church and the City can render.

The first service which the Church in fact can and should render to the commercial community — and it is one about which the Scriptures are uncomfortably explicit — is to stress the grave spiritual dangers that lie in wait for anyone whose chief activity is the accumulation and manipulation of wealth. Some are of course obvious, the temptations to avarice, pride, deceit and so on. But in the captialist economy in which we have grown up there is a deeper error which lies behind all these and which is more difficult to discern, namely the mistaking of abstractions for concrete realities and the consequent confusion of means and ends. If we ask, as people hardly ever trouble to do, what is the legitimate purpose of a financial system, the answer should be something like this: it is to encourage and facilitate the production, distribution and exchange of material goods in ways which will best respect the safety and welfare of human beings and the conservation of the world's resources. What we have in fact is a system in which the primary purpose of the system is the production of financial profit; and money, instead of being a mechanism for the achievement of the beneficent ends just mentioned, is primarily a mechanism for the production of more money, an abstraction breeding abstractions.

Of course, if the experts confined themselves entirely to the abstract realm of make-believe, no particular harm would be done, any more than, when people playing Monopoly buy and sell imaginary property in Fleet Street or the Strand, anything happens to the real buildings and their activities. The matter is very difficult when speculators buy and sell corn or butter or merely trade dollars for marks, for, although they themselves may never see the commodites which they buy and sell, and these may even not exist, their speculations may affect the life and health of men, women and children on the other side of the world, for whom corn and butter are not tokens in a financial game but the necessities for their physical life. Judged by its ability to fulfil the proper purposes of an economic order capitalism can only be condemned as monstrously inefficient, but this is hardly surprising in view of the fact that it has been designed and operated for an entirely different purpose, namely the production of financial profit for its investors. The naive assumption that by some occult mechanism it will providentially satisfy both purposes simultaneously has not surprisingly been badly disappointed. The alternation of booms and slumps on a world scale, with all its accompaniments of human misery, and the near-breakdown of the whole system through the mounting and apparently insoluble indebtedness of the Third World are two of its most alarming features; but perhaps the clearest demonstration of its sheer irrationality is provided by the common phenomenon of the development of a backward area by a transnational corporation producing high-quality goods for export with an actual lowering of the standard of living of the producers, who find the products entirely beyond their means.

I would recommend, as a useful antidote to the moralism and complacency with which we in the more favoured countries find it easy to lull our consciences, a careful reading of the following passage from an article written, by a demographic expert based on Darjeeling, shortly after the recent United Nations Conference on Human Environment in

Stockholm (its substance, though drawn from India, could be paralleled by material from most other parts of the Third World):

> Personally, I am angered at reading the pompous declaration of yet one more international conference on forestry while daily I see a stream of peasants with a pile of newly chopped trees on their heads, taking it to market to sell or to use for their own cooking. Yet, knowing all this and the futility of attempting to stop this daily destruction, the government makes not one serious move to provide an alternative fuel. Or, again from India, that country must be the largest producer of cow-dung in the world, since its cattle produce little else, yet instead of being used for enriching the soil, it is burnt as fuel. One cannot blame the poor, who in their poverty have no thought of even tomorrow but only of how to live today. Meanwhile, as Barbara Ward says in the same context, the favoured nations do 'regard the universe as expendable — as long as their tiny bit of it is not expended . . . There is a curious tension between what governments subconsciously know to be the international realities and what they are prepared to accept in limitation of their sovereign interests. Too often it is still *my* earth, only *one hundred* earths'.
>
> What is said of nations goes equally for classes and castes within the nation who mercilessly exploit their economic advantage. What is said about environmental issues applies equally to the population problems: it is possible to correct the imbalance between resources and demographic growth; the means, e.g., of producing sufficient food are known, but the obstacles of doing so are, for the most part, to be found elsewhere than in agriculture itself. The prices offered to farmers are too low to encourage greater production; it is the rich farmers, who have the capital, who profit by the green revolution; while the subsistence farmers, with a few acres of infertile land, are pushed still further down the ladder. If, furthermore inefficiency is endemic, corruption widespread and an adequate infrastructure of development is wanting, the causes of our problems are legion. *It is a sad, sad world that cannot supply adequate food, clothing, shelter or even an unpolluted cup of water to half its population.* To lay the blame for such a situation totally on population increase . . . is the sheerest nonsense, but useful as a cover for the covetousness and greed of the rich in both the North and the South.[9]

In the face of a situation such as is here described it is difficult to understand how anyone who believes that the central point of Christian belief is that the maker of the universe is now a man can claim that the Church ought to have nothing to do with politics. And before it is too hastily assumed that the words 'rich' and 'poor' simply carry the connotation that they have in British party politics it is well to remember that the workers on tea plantations in Sri Lanka were quoted in 1977 as being paid from 11 to 14 *dollars per month*,[10] a wage which would hardly

---

9. Albert Nevett, S. J., 'People and Resources: a reappraisal', *The Month*, May 1983, p. 164, (italics mine).
10. 'The Case against Capitalism', A. F. McGovern, *Marxism: An American Christian Perspective*, Maryknoll N.Y., Orbis Books 1980, p. 145, where other examples of wages in the Third World are given.

satisfy the British workers, with their televisions and foreign holidays, who depend so much on the product of the Lankans' toil for their own creature comforts. (In saying this I do not imply that there is no serious poverty in Britain or that the existing social services are adequate to cope with it.)

One of the most vital, and at the same time controversial, movements in the Church today is that of the Liberation Theology which is associated particularly with Latin America and of which the best known writings are those by Gustavo Gutiérrez, Juan Luis Segundo, Jon Sabrino and Leonardo Boff. It is, I think, impossible for any socially sensitive Christian not to feel admiration for their championship of the exploited and impoverished masses in their lands and indignation at the tacit alliance which existed until recently (and is still not everywhere extinct) between the ecclesiastical establishment and the ruthless organisation of transnational capitalist finance. But what I find extremely puzzling is that the Liberation theologians fail almost entirely to recognise that all the justification which is needed for their revolt is already to be found in the existing corpus of Catholic doctrine, however scandalously many high ecclesiastics have shut their eyes to it. It does not need for its formulation some up-dated version of Marxism as many Liberation theologians seem to think. And any notion that the obviously reserved attitude of Pope John Paul to liberation theology implies repudiation of active concern for social righteousness, or even an implicit blessing of the agencies of exploitation and repression, should be utterly demolished by such an utterance as the following which he made at the beginning of 1979 in the republic of San Domingo:

> The Church . . . wishes today to continue her mission of faith and defence of human rights, inviting all Christians to devote themselves to the construction of a world that is more just, more human, more habitable, which is not closed in on itself but open to God. To make this world more just means, among other things, making sure that there are no children without food, without education and without religious instruction, that there are no young people without appropriate training, that there are no peasants without land to live on where they may develop with dignity, that there are no workers ill-treated or with their rights curtailed, that there are no systems which allow for the exploitation of man by man or by the State, that there is no corruption, that there is no superabundance of riches for some and undeserved poverty for others, that there are no families disrupted, disunited or disregarded, that there is no injustice and inequality in the implementation of justice, that there is no one without the protection of the law, and that the law protects all equally, that force does not prevail over truth and right but rather that truth and right prevail over force, that economics and politics do not smother humanity.[11]

11. *The Tablet*, Feb. 3, 1979, p. 98.

Communists may have demanded less than this for humanity, but have they ever demanded more?

A fully conscious and explicit acceptance of the universal character of the human nature of the incarnate Lord will have an immediate bearing upon the Church's missionary propaganda. It will mean that each of the various human cultures will have its own distinctive contribution to make to the understanding and the expression of the revelation given by God to mankind in Jesus. This, it must be stressed, is the precise opposite of the kind of religious relativism and syncretism of such writers as Dr D. E. Nineham and Dr John Hick, according to whom the various world-religions, including Christianity, are variously differentiated culturally conditioned expressions of a basic human religious urge which, in the tolerant atmosphere of liberal democracy, may hopefully anticipate a peaceful reconciliation. It will insist on an uncompromising assertion of the unique incarnation of God in Christ and an equal confidence in the power of that unique incarnation to release and perfect the hidden potentialities of each several people and culture. I will illustrate this point by the testimony of an Anglican priest, John Davies, after fourteen years in South Africa. In Africa, he writes,

> A form of Christianity which takes incarnation seriously speaks and registers. Incarnation is a gospel, not an embarrassment. Christ present in the sacrament, Christ present in the community, Christ present in the person of the priest — all this has made converting and sanctifying sense . . . The most powerful weapon in Catholicism's armoury of imagery in the struggle against injustice is the doctrine of the Body of Christ. There has been nothing radical or intellectually daring about this: the South African situation has required Catholicism to be thoroughly conservative and oppose the novel nonsense of upstart racism with a traditional orthodoxy which insists that there must be a visible fellowship of believers and that Christian love must be acted out in visible terms. South African apartheid ideology is Eutychian. It says that the love and fellowship of Christian belief is a spiritual reality and need not be visible in structure or meeting . . . An incarnational faith will insist that this is reversing the gospel; instead of representing a word that becomes flesh it is removing people from flesh into a world only of words. The doctrine of the Body of Christ insists that the love of God must continue to be embodied, made visible, verifiable, even structured. This has been the central message of the Catholic tradition, and it has been received with enthusiasm by blacks — who of course go on to ask us to show the evidence for our witness!

And again:

> There are some elements in Catholic doctrine which are of great importance, in which contact can be made with an African world view to an extent which the missionaries could not have realised at first. The most obvious of these is the doctrine of the Communion of Saints: and, even more important, because it is

more Christologically central, is the doctrine of the descent of Christ into Hell. Most central of all, a Church which truly insists on the doctrine of the Trinity will, if it is patient, discover that Africa can not only receive it but renew it in a fresh disclosure. The doctrine of the Trinity is, in part, an account of how, at the heart of things, the power-principle is subordinated to the community-principle, and how the shared properties of personhood are related to the distinct and unique features of individuality.

I must refrain from quoting at greater length from John Davies's superb exposition, but I must add one passage which bears directly on our present subject of the relation between religion and politics:

> The Catholic doctrine of the communion of saints enables us to take our ancestral identities seriously. A Christianity which fails to teach this doctrine can do little about our racial, national or tribal consciousness except tell us to grow out of it, be ashamed of it, or suppress it. Catholicism can recognise that our racial consciousness is indeed part of our created nature; but it also insists that in Christ's descent to Hell he has healed the antagonisms which made our ancestors enemies of each other, and that the Christian altar is the meeting place of all the human race, living and departed, in all their ancestral identities. Christ enables racial enemies to meet as neighbours; the Church is the place where people of different cultures meet their one Lord, because the Church stands for the destruction of those patterns of injustice which elevate one group into a supposed superiority over another.[12]

The longest, and one of the last to be promulgated, of the Documents of the Second Vatican Council is the Pastoral Constitution of the Church in the World of Today.[13] Partly because of the word 'Pastoral' in its title and partly, it may be, because of its very length, people have often overlooked its solid doctrinal substance. Such an impression is firmly corrected by the thorough study made by an Indian priest, Fr George Karakunnel of the Gregorian University in Rome. He shows that, although it took as its starting-point the actual concrete situation and condition of man in this present-day world, the Constitution's own thinking has the twofold theme of man as made in God's image to rule over the world and man as the creature whose nature God himself has assumed — Man as the Image of God, and Man in the Mystery of Christ. And because the Incarnation is a genuine and permanent reality, Christ is both the centre of the world-process and its future climax and consummation. History and eschatology both receive their meaning in Christ.

Thus, Fr Karakunnel maintains, the whole Constitution has an anthropological-Christological structure. Its approach is indeed novel:

---

12. John Davies, "The Catholic Movement for export", in *Essays Catholic and Radical*, edd. Kenneth Leech and Rowan Williams, Bowerdean Press 1983, pp. 188ff, 190, 192.
13. *Gaudium et Spes*, Dec. 7, 1965.

'The Constitution employs an inductive method gathering concrete facts . . . The present context of man's history becomes the frame of the Council's thinking.' But 'its theological vision is something that time will not change.' What it provides is 'Creative Utilisation of Christian Sources and a New Development of Christian Doctrine.' The Sources are what they have always been: Scripture, the Fathers, the Tradition of the Church. There is no concession to those 'new Christologies' which see Jesus as simply a man who was uniquely endowed with the Spirit of God; nothing less is offered to man, perplexed as he is about his own significance and lost among forces which he feels more and more powerless to control, than the traditional Gospel that the Creator of the universe has entered into his own creation, becoming what we are in order that we might become what he is. But it is equally clear that the implications of this truth and the consequences of that event have been only very partially seen, especially in the social and political sphere. It is in this sense that the Constitution called for a new development of Christian Doctrine and made the first steps in such a development.

Theologians have never found it easy to relate together in a balanced and systematic way the Church's concern with the establishment of peace and justice upon earth and the final transfiguration and transformation in Christ at the Last Day. As Fr Karakunnel points out, the Constitution shows an edifying combination of confidence and reticence on the subject:

> We do not know the time for the consummation of the earth and of humanity, nor do we know how all things are transformed. As deformed by sin the shape of this world passes away. But we are taught that God is preparing a new dwelling and a new earth where justice will abide and whose beatitude will fulfil and conquer all the desires of peace which rise in the hearts of men. Then, with death overcome, the sons of God will be raised up in Christ and what was sown in weakness and corruption will put on incorruption . . .
>
> The expectation of a new earth should not weaken but rather stimulate our concern to cultivate this one, since there grows here the body of a new human family which even now can give some kind of adumbration of the new age.[14]

And it is in the sacramental life of the Church, and especially in the Eucharist, that the transformation of the created world in Christ is both prefigured and anticipated:

> The Lord has left his people a pledge of hope and food for their journey in that Sacrament of faith in which natural elements, worked on by man, are changed

14. *Gaudium et Spes,* 39.

> into his glorious Body and Blood, providing a meal of brotherly solidarity and a foretaste of the heavenly banquet.[15]

Fr Karakunnel stresses the deliberately open and unfinished character of the Constitution. Unlike many official documents, it was not intended to conclude discussion but rather to initiate it. It falls organically in line with the stream of great papal social encyclicals stretching back to *Rerum Novarum* of Leo XIII in 1891 and coming down, through *Quadragesimo Anno* of Pius XI forty years later, *Mater et Magistra* and *Pacem in Terris* of John XXIII and *Populorum Progressio* of Paul VI, to *Redemptor Hominis, Dives in Misericordia* and *Laborem Exercens* of the present Supreme Pastor John Paul II, the last having been prepared for the ninetieth anniversary of Leo's great initiative.

Reverting now to the position in this situation of the Anglican Churches, I may perhaps be allowed to end on a personal note. It is just fifty years since I was ordained as a priest in the Church of England; it is also just fifty years since we were celebrating the centenary of the Catholic revival in that Church. It was also the time of the great Anglo-Catholic congresses and of a tremendous sense of optimism on both the theological and the practical plane. Its most vocal expression was given by what came to be known as the Christendom group from the journal in which most of its writings appeared; it was composed of such well established, though, in the eyes of the ecclesiastical establishment, dangerous, figures as P. E. T. Widdrington, M. B. Reckitt, W. G. Peck and V. A. Demant, and a number of younger people who clustered round them. The Group was certainly not peaceful (it continued through the time of the Jarrow hunger marches and the Spanish Civil War!), but what held it together and distinguished it from other social and political movements that claimed to be broadly 'Christian' was the conviction that the leading principles for social and political activity by Christians are the direct consequences of the Catholic doctrines of the nature, predicament and resources of man.

We made many mistakes and were the object of many criticisms, both just and unjust, but we firmly held that there was a Christian sociology and that it was derived from, and indeed was really part of, Christian belief. In many ways the place which the Christendom Group held has now been taken by the oddly-named 'Jubilee Group', which has published its own volume *Essays Catholic and Radical* to celebrate the

---

15. *Gaudium et Spes*. 38, Fr Karakunnel's masterly study, hitherto unpublished is deposited in the Gregorian University.

150th anniversary of the Catholic revival. Its editors, Kenneth Leach and Rowan Williams, in their Introduction, stress the need of a *critical* orthodoxy and in particular of a *theological* critique of capitalism and they voice disquiet and anxiety at the present failure of Anglican Catholics to meet it. In this I seem almost to hear the echo of our own voices fifty years ago!

The protest is always needed, against complacency and self-interest, but without, I hope, substituting my own type of complacency I would utter a warning against a type of error which in the Christendom Group we did on the whole manage to avoid. I mean the error of thinking of political issues primarily in terms of right and left. 'Right' and 'left' are political, not theological, categories, derived, I believe, from the seating-arrangements of continental parliaments, and I think they came into common use here about the time of the Spanish Civil War. To introduce them into Christian thinking about social questions tends to set up false polarisations and to obscure the real and relevant distinctions that need to be made.

Postscript

Many years ago Jacques Maritain wrote *La Primauté du Spirituel*; it was translated into English as *The Things that are not Caesar's*. Has anyone given a book the title *The Things that are not God's?*

Eric Mascall is Emeritus professor of historical theology at the University of London.

3
Why go to church?

Graham Turner

I, and many millions like me, owe an immeasurable debt to the Church of England. If not the author of my faith, it feeds, renews and sustains the faith as little else can. After a week marked by confusion, difficulty and error, a week when my life has always fallen well short of the best, it is a great relief to kneel in the simple parish church and let the majesty and incisiveness of the liturgy convict, cleanse and comfort my soul. As we say together the words of the Eucharist . . . 'we are not worthy so much as to gather up the crumbs under Thy table . . . that we may evermore dwell in Him and He in us . . . therefore with angels and archangels and all the company of Heaven . . . we offer Thee our souls and bodies to be a living sacrifice', I feel a whirling universe being steadied and my life brought back towards its true centre. Nor is it just for the place and the words that I feel gratitude. I feel grateful for faithful priests who speak the liturgy with reverence and grace, even on winter evenings when there are only half a dozen to hear; who hold out the hand of the eternal to us amid life's most searing tragedies; and for their wives, who endure chilly vicarages, where a coal-fire is sometimes a weekly treat, and wear the best second-hand clothes they can afford.

In one way, too, I love the Church of England for its spirit of restraint. It is a spirit which looks askance at zealotry; which dislikes being button-holed or quizzed about its beliefs; and disapproves of those who offer us rapturous hallelujahs in public places of worship. All of that, in so many ways, suits my particular temperament. Whether, by itself, it would meet my needs is a very different matter. For I have to say, sadly, that there is a great deal which the Church of England does *not* do for me, and for which I have to look elsewhere. As an ordinary pew-person, who longs that in some small way his life may mirror the love of Christ, the first thing I need is effective help with my imperfections. Sin is a short and disagreeable word but, unless I belong to the sort of fellowship where I am helped, regularly and concretely, to be honest about my sins and to see how to deal with them, then I steadily become a dead soul, attending the services, assenting to the ritual, but dead; and am neither able to go in peace nor serve the Lord, both of which the Eucharist enjoins me to do. In other words, the same Church which wills the end does not (in my case) also provide the means.

Here I have to confess to some puzzlement. Does the Church of England reckon to help its members deal with their sins, aside, that is from general exhortations to goodness from the pulpit — rather in the manner of an optician dispensing eye-medicine from a second-story window — plus the long-term, beneficial effect of the liturgy? Powerful as the liturgy is, to expect that combination to deal concretely with the entrenched egoism of the human will, and send it forth to fight Christ's battle in the world, is the ultimate in optimism.

There is, for example, the general confession. Well, how effective is a *general* confession? I can only speak for myself. In me, it often produces a general sense of remorse and, occasionally, the painful recollection of some gross error; but, since it so rarely pinpoints a specific sin, it equally rarely leads to atonement for that sin. My own experience is that *particular* confession, whether to a trusted friend or a priest, and on the basis of the absolute standards of honesty, purity, unselfishness and love which Jesus sets for us, is infinitely more effective, because it exposes my gruesome behaviour to the glaring, shaming light of day. If I have to spell out, *alfresco* and not *sub rosa*, exactly how I lost my temper with my wife, over what trivial incident the explosion occurred, what sort of language I used — or, for that matter, how I failed to give a friend the challenge which God had asked me to set before him, then I have to look my callousness or cowardice full in the face, and there is at least a chance that remorse will turn to repentance, God's healing grace flow in. And that the whole experience will be so searing that I shall not repeat that particular error in a hurry!

Without regular fellowship of that sort, barnacles grow on my soul. Yet I wonder how many Anglican churches reckon to provide that kind of freeing, feeding fellowship? How many priests, or laymen for that matter, arc surgeons of souls, ready to engage in the messy but infinitely fruitful work of helping individuals face up to their natures and find freedom? How many spend adequate time (indeed, any time) seeking from the Holy Spirit the moral key which will bring individual souls to new life (like the friend who asked me the infuriating, but life-changing question 'So you think personal ambition is a good thing, do you?')

How many feel they could never find the time to do such work, amid the draining graft of keeping an institution ticking over (and why on earth do we swamp our priests with financial drudgery and committee chores, expecting them to be both minister and manager, yogi and commissar?) How many priests, dare I ask, even open themselves enough, save for the cursory acknowledgement of fellow-sinner status from the pulpit, to win the confidence of their parishioners? Some, as I know from personal experience, do. There is a priest in Oxford who has, in his study, a settee with a dent at either end, the one made by himself, the other by a succession of young men and women with whom he has had personal, and often life-changing talks. Again, in a tiny parish in Sussex, there is another Anglican priest who, in Malcolm Muggeridge's view, is a saint. There are people in that parish who have decided not to move house merely because he is there. The reasons are simple enough. An uncloying love, the gift of Christ and the fruit of an obedient life, pours out of him; he is devout but entirely free both of bogus piosity and sweaty enthusiasm; and he opens his heart so freely to his parishioners that it seems the most natural thing in the world for them to share the deepest things on *their* hearts in return. The result is that, in that church, you can see people growing spiritually.

Too few, however, earn the right — by the quality and openness of their lives — to do that work, or indeed try to do it. They are thoroughly dutiful and immensely hard-working, but they are not the sort of men to whom you feel you could talk candidly about the things of which you are most ashamed, or even the ordinary errors and dilemmas of everyday life. Would they not, you wonder, be too busy? Might it not be a burden to them? Might they not even be embarrassed? They are not, in other words, at grips with the real lives of their parishioners, with the moral problems which beset pew-people like me, the thorns-in-flesh which defeat us. Hence, as it seems to me, they often lack the challenge and the reality to which the young, in particular, respond.

'There's definitely no militancy about the Church of England', said a student in Oxford, 'and never any directness between our vicar and the congregation. If you were having an affair with somebody, you're not going to be bothered by him. I don't think he's been trained to get down to that sort of thing, and nobody seems to want him to anyway. He never really tackles the nitty-gritty of our lives'. His sister, then away at boarding school, had a similar reaction. 'At least half the girls don't want to go to church', she said. 'After all, we get some pretty grotty preachers. They very rarely talk about things that are real to girls like us — things like gossiping and stealing and broken homes — they only go on about general things like "God is love". You just sit there and think "Great!" '

'I don't think the Church of England is likely to give anyone a faith unless they've got one already', agreed her mother, herself an enthusiastic Anglican. 'There's no attack about it. So many of the priests don't seem to believe in actually influencing people. They just leave them alone and hope it gets through. They also don't expect to be personal unless they're dealing with someone's grief'.

But, a priest might fairly ask, how many of the people facing him in the pew *want* him to help them deal with their personal shortcomings? How would they react if he *did* begin to deal with the nitty-gritty? Both are valid questions. As laymen, we need to ask what we go to church for. How many of us simply want to drink in as much as we are able to from the liturgy, but otherwise prefer not to have our own lives disturbed? A good many, of course, are truly devout — and Anglican devotion carries itself with an unassuming grace which is highly attractive — but others among us roll up expecting to give (and, it seems, to receive) very little.

'I've really no idea why people go to church', admitted one churchwarden. 'Maybe it's a form of insurance. Being the churchwarden, I perhaps ought not to say this, but I'm not all that sure why I go myself.' 'I go because I wouldn't be happy if I didn't', said the wife of a consultant in a lively and highly 'successful' parish north of London. 'Problems come up which you can't always sort out, and it's vital for me to go to church regularly so I can think them out in a calm frame of mind'. She is as worried by other members of the congregation showing too much friendliness as too little. 'I used to be terribly afraid that someone would come up and ask if I believed in God', she murmured, 'and then having to say "sorry, I don't think so"'.

The Church of England is a broad church and long may it so remain, but parishioners of this kind, particularly when encountered in bulk, can have a crushing effect on a priest's heart. If parts of the Church of England are spiritually comatose, a large slice of the blame lies with half-hearted laymen who have had no real spiritual experience themselves and tend to douse any fire which may burn within a priest. I talked recently to a young rector in a Cheshire industrial town, and asked what his congregation said after he had preached a sermon. Nothing at all, he replied, they just leave. 'If I preached an enthusiastic sermon', he added, 'they'd think I'd gone round the bend'. He had suggested that, for the church's patronal festival, each member of the congregation might bring a friend to morning or evening service. But not one had. He loved his job, said the rector, but it was lonely. Sometimes he felt like the captain of the *Marie Celeste*, as if all the crew had gone and he was the only one left. It sounded to me as if he will either have to go out and bring an experience of Christ to new people or else drift off into the sunset with his present skeleton crew.

This, of course, is a picture of a moribund church, and much of the Church of England is far from moribund. Many parishes flourish. There are signs of a return to faith in many places. In my own parish, there are regular baptisms and confirmations of people of 'mature' years. Yet, unless the church provides the kind of fellowship where it can naturally get down to the nitty-gritty of people's lives, it will not play the part in our communities and nation which it should. The engine of real growth in any church is sins faced and forgiven: lives set free. If that work is not done, then too much of the Church of England will remain bland and under-powered, offering at best, half a gospel.

'Its role', said a Northern housewife who loves the Church of England, but sometimes despairs of it too, 'is to provide a house of God for people with a faith who don't particularly want to talk about it. It's basically the English method of making sure that the noxious fumes of religion don't overcome anybody, of stunning religion so it can't be effective. It's the religious expression of that tremendous English reserve which means you don't smile at anybody in trains. The Church of England only causes trouble these days when it meddles in political things. It never causes any trouble by its religious activities, because everybody is at great pains to make the whole thing as bland as possible. Salt? It's more like arrowroot, it doesn't taste of anything very much'.

So, in my own personal life, the Church of England, as I have experienced it, does not even begin to meet my need. It provides the bread of life, but not the salt which should go with it. It feeds me but it does not cleanse me. There is a second area, equally important, where it also fails me. Given that I have faith, which I do, what sort of vision does it set before me of the way I am meant to express my Christianity in my daily life? Or rather, what help does it give me in discovering that vision?

I see many inspiring things going on around me in the Church. I see retired ladies serving the old, the sick and the under-privileged with great love and devotion. I see other ladies offering their services in a variety of other ways — for example, in providing and arranging flowers, which they do beautifully — while their husbands tend the churchyard. I am invited to ecumenical services with the Methodists, and to deanery Eucharists. I am invited to contribute to the church in Zululand, and to a wide range of other missions. I am invited to join with the rest of the congregation in praying that our leaders may be given wisdom from above.

I do not undervalue any of these things. They are all concrete expressions of a love of Christ, and of a desire to express that love by being of service to others. Having said that, I am left wondering what challenge and vision the Church offers to those involved in the world of work and even, as in my own case (if only as an observer), in public life?

What does it say to us, for example, about the part we might be able to play in making Britain the Christian nation it ought to be? Does it provoke us to consider whether, in addition to our missions to the Zulu and the Matabele, some of us ought to feel a sense of mission to (for instance) those in public life? Who, after all, takes the trouble to think and care and fight for those people? Have so many of our politicians, to take one example, been lucky enough to have had the same experience as some of us, of the Holy Spirit showing us how to clean up our grubby lives and start out on a new road? On the contrary, I would have thought one of the most striking features of our national political leadership is how very, very few reckon to put God first in their lives — and that goes for all parties. So, do these men and women need our care and friendship less than our brothers in distant lands? And, if not, who is going to befriend them and help them find new life? Who is going to set before them a vision of how they might serve our nation and the world if the Holy Spirit had full right of way in their hearts? Who is going to do for them what men like Isaac Milner, the Cambridge academic, and John Newton, the former slave captain, did for William Wilberforce, which helped him become the greatest Christian statesman of his age?

The same spiritual poverty is evident in every part of our national life. Who would say, for example, that our business and trade union leaders are any less in need? Who would claim that, because of the vision they have been given by the Church or the new life they have found through it, we now have a couple of dozen leading industrialists painfully pioneering with their colleagues an answer to unemployment under the guidance of the Holy Spirit? Equally, who would say that there are half-a-dozen trade union leaders discovering that new vision for their organisations which God might entrust to men whose hearts were wholly given to Him? Are we in the Church helping them find that new life? Does the Church send us out to take on that kind of task?

Again, I can speak only for myself. I may have missed a great deal which the Church of England has to offer, but the plain truth is that I have had to look outside it for the two visions which have inspired me most: namely, the aim of helping to build a Britain governed by men and women governed by God, and the notion that, as Christians, our task under god is nothing less than the remaking of the world. Both are challenges well beyond me, which take me into a dimension where only the power of God is adequate; both, perhaps for that very reason, stir my heart; and both make me *want* all the more to offer my life.

I have no doubt that there are many prelates and priests who help their parishioners discover that kind of vision. For example I know a rector in a parish near Reading who, when he gazes down at his congregation on Sunday, tries to visualise what they will all be doing on Monday morning, so that he may think of them in his quiet moments of reflection, not merely as servants of the Church, potential sidesmen or Sunday School teachers, but as men and women for whom God has a very special destiny in the great world outside, and who may need his help to fulfil that destiny. It is a different attitude from those who envisage greater Christian commitment as meaning organising a new stewardship campaign. Listening to my friend in Reading talk made me wonder how many priests have an even greater vision for what their parishioners might do *outside* the church than inside it. How many, indeed, know enough about that outside world to be able adequately to live into the lives of their parishioners? How many inhabit what is essentially a religious ghetto, where they act as quasi-social workers during the week and pray for the Queen on Sundays? I well remember an ex-Communist friend of mine saying that if Anglicans were as dedicated and effective as the Marxists with whom he had previously been working, the face of Britain would be entirely different.

Equally, I have not forgotten the candid remarks of a canon's wife in the Midlands about the nature of some of their church activities. 'We've got a Young Wives Group', she said, 'and it's a nice gathering, but it's not a religious thing at all. The subject may be interesting, but it's usually nothing to do with the Christian life. What does it do? It's a rather self-perpetuating circle of busyness within the Church. To them, I'm afraid, "more committed" means doing the flowers more often or joining the Mothers' Union. It has very little to do with fighting Christ's battle in the world.'

But, then, might not the same be said for the performance of many of the Church's leaders over these last decades? In some ways, they have been years of pronounced moral decline. We now have 162,000 abortions a year, two millions in total under the current law, and one does not need to take a pro-Life position to regard that statistic as a deep stain on our national character, not to mention the souls of those who have treated the disposal of nascent human life, their own flesh and blood, as a matter of convenience. At the same time, we have seen divorce tearing through our society like a tidal wave, and leaving behind its tragic infant flotsam. We have seen simulated buggery on the stage, and homosexual lust flaunting itself around the world alongside its heterosexual counterpart under the 'Gay' banner.

Small wonder that John Baker, Bishop of Salisbury, should declare that anyone transported from the 1950s to the 1980s by time-capsule would think they were in Sodom. His confessor at Cuddesdon in the 1950s he recalled, had told him that the bulk of the Church of England were not living in the real world and that, if Baker could hear the same confessions as he did, he would realise that the dam was already breached, the war lost. His, declared Baker, had been a prophetic voice.

So, how have the Anglican episcopate matched up to the challenge? Have they, as one might have expected, behaved like a herd of enraged elephants thundering and trumpeting about the land? Not to my ears, at least. Instead, there has been a curious silence, punctuated only by the shuffling of feet. During breaks in the silence, Anglican 'divines' could be heard debating the existence of God, ruminating on whether Jesus might not have been homosexual and cooking up prayers for use after abortions: 'Into Your Hands we commit in trust the life which we have just cut short'. Some bishops are apt to claim that they have been trumpeting away in their own little corners and that the media have simply failed to record their blasts. All one can say is that not a single one of them has earned national recognition as a trumpeter against moral decadence. To their shame, the only person to win that accolade has been not a prelate but a lay-woman, Mrs Mary Whitehouse, who strode in where so many bishops feared even to tiptoe.

So, why the lack of prophet voices? Did Anglican bishops not care what was happening in our society? That, one would have thought, is most unlikely. Many of them, after all, have been good and devout men. Far more likely, perhaps, that they were suffering from what Eric Wild, former Bishop of Reading, calls 'a curious lack of authentic Christian confidence'. Even that diagnosis, however, still begs the question: whence the timidity and the uncertainty. One reason why the bishops have not taken more of a stand over the last 20 years, according to John Baker, is what he calls 'the chaotic state of doctrinal and moral theology' within all the Protestant churches. In other words, on many issues the Church of England no longer knows what it *does* believe. It cannot even decide, as Baker points out, how it wants to use the Bible. The fact that the Bible is no longer the Church's guide-line and bench-mark is only too evident from the views advanced by some of our leading bishops on a subject such as homosexuality. If a priest brought a 'friend' to live with him in the vicarage, said John Bickersteth, Bishop of Bath and Wells, that was a matter of scandal. If the cleric kept his male friend off the patch, say in London, that was a matter for his own conscience. Out of sight, it seems, out of mind.

John Habgood, Archbishop of York, takes a similar line. We are, he says, learning to be 'more relaxed' about such matters, while (of course) maintaining the standards we have always had. For example, where a priest had a male 'lodger', he was not going to inquire too closely what happened in the privacy of that home. After all, we didn't make judgements about the quality of each other's marriages, did we? In his eyes, apparently, homosexual liaisons and marriages come to much the same thing. But then, he says, we know a lot more about 'the condition of homosexuality' than St Paul did. All one can say for poor old St Paul is that, in the light of the AIDS epidemic now afflicting the 'gay' community in the United States, he at least got the consequence of homosexual practice right when he predicted that it would reap 'that recompense of their error which was meet'. In the light of that epidemic, furthermore, one asks oneself who shows more love for homosexuals: St Paul, who condemns such practices outright, or Anglican clerics who murmur about more relaxed attitudes?

There are other reasons for the lack of forthrightness which so many of our bishops have shown. For one thing, they do not like to appear foolish by being too far out of step with the times. 'If bishops had laid down the law', Gerald Ellison, former Bishop of London, remarked to me, 'people would have said "these men don't know the world we're living in"'. Had Jesus or St Paul taken the same stance, Christianity would not have deserved even a mention in history. Bishops, Ellison went on, didn't like to commit themselves to anything which would make them look silly. For instance, he certainly hadn't wanted to be known as the anti-striptease bishop. He'd preferred to work quietly in Soho.

Then take the Pope, setting his face against so many things which he believed to be sinful, yet disobeyed by so many of his followers. So what, say I? At least he is in the tradition of Jesus and can honestly claim to be the Vicar of Christ, not the Vicar of the Crawling Consensus. But Ellison is an honest and honourable man who candidly admits that the bishops have little reason to be proud of their record over the last 20 years. 'I think', he said, 'that we have reflected the uncertainties which prevail everywhere'. But what about the eternal certainties? Had they reflected those enough? 'An absolutely fair observation', replied Ellison. 'I don't think I did speak out adequately'. He had, for example, agreed with Mary Whitehouse when she had prosecuted the National Theatre over simulated homosexual scenes in Howard Brenton's *Romans in Britain*. But had he said so, I asked? 'That', replied Ellison, 'is a very leading question. I don't know if I had an opportunity'.

Others failed to take a stand because they felt helpless. John Wakeling, Bishop of Southwell and a most charming and humble man, has been, and is, wholly against the flood-tide of abortions. Why then, had he not said so? 'Partly', he admitted, 'because people would have asked me what I was going to do about it'. A clergy wife whom I met at a lunch party given by the Bishop of Worcester in Hartlebury Castle diagnosed the episcopal malaise more simply. The trouble with bishops, she declared bluntly, 'is that they want to be loved by everybody, and they can't be'. So far as I can see, many of them want not only to be liked by us but actually to be *like* us.

When I meet a bishop, or indeed any cleric, I want to find not a mirror of myself but a miracle of God; not someone who lights up his fourth Embassy Tipped of the morning but someone who, by his evident holiness, challenges me afresh to live the life of the Cross. Christ was *God* with us, as well as man with us — and our clergy are meant to be Christ's representatives on earth, or they are nothing.

I want them to be not diffident ditherers and man-pleasers but men of authority, an authority authenticated by the lives they lead. I want them to be not men who make their name by taking a 'progressive' line on secular issues but men who gain their reputation helping others find new life. Too often, in my experience, our clerics' conception of love is of something soft and compromising. They seem to forget that Jesus called people 'a nest of vipers' and 'whited sepulchres' — and that that, *too*, is the language of love, a Love which knew that to let men live on in sin is itself a sin, the sin of utter callousness.

So let us have at our head godly men, with all the joy and humour which that brings; battling men, who behave like soldiers of Christ, not conscientious objectors to the Gospel. Then if we laymen and laywomen played our part, Britain would have cause to be grateful to the Church of England, that church of martyrs and poets, saints and scholars, which is meant to stand for God's truth at the heart of this nation and which millions of us hold so very dear.

Graham Turner is a journalist working for the Sunday Telegraph.

4
Doctored doctrine

Michael Moreton

What is the basis of doctrine in the Church of England? The Constitutions and Canons Ecclesiastical of 1603, in the manner of the times, briskly censured those who impugned the Book of Common Prayer, the Articles of Religion, the Rites and Ceremonies of the Church of England, and the form and manner of making and consecrating Bishops, Priests and Deacons, as being superstitious, erroneous, and contrary to the Word of God. Such impugners were to be excommunicated *ipso facto*, and not to be restored until they should repent and publicly revoke such wicked errors.[1] The revised canons of our own times, however, display a different temper. Censure is eschewed, and a more complaisant tone is favoured. Thus, in the Proposals for a Revised Body of Canons contained in the Report, *The Canon Law of the Church of England*, the Thirty-nine Articles of Religion, the Book of Common Prayer, and the Ordinal were declared to be agreeable to the Word of God, and hence might be subscribed and used with a good conscience. Further, the doctrine of the Church of England was said to be 'grounded in the Holy Scriptures and in the teaching of the ancient Fathers and Councils of the Church, and is particularly contained in the Thirty-nine Articles of Religion, the Book of Common Prayer, and the Ordinal'.[2] When these Proposals were revised and authorised, however, a note of reservation was sounded. Article A.5 now reads: 'The doctrine of the Church of England is grounded in the Holy Scriptures and in *such teachings* of the ancient Fathers and Councils of the Church *as are agreeable to the said Scriptures*'.[3] And so the case now stands.

With the Book of Common Prayer the Church of England has been balanced on a knife edge. Different schools of theological thought have

1. *Constitutions and Canons Ecclesiastical,* 1603, nos. 4-8.
2. *The Canon Law of the Church of England,* SPCK 1947, canons II-V, pp. 106f.
3. *Canon Law Revision 1959*, SPCK 1960, p. 10 (our italic).

learned to live with it, taking advantage of its ambiguities and lacunae. But its revision, as 1928 showed, was likely to bring out into the open the theological contradictions within the Church of England, and to precipitate the alienation of some for whom the BCP made life tolerable. The appearance of the Alternative Service Book has certainly occasioned controversy, but hitherto on literary rather than theological grounds. Yet, as this essay will seek to indicate, the ASB diverges from the BCP in doctrine in a number of ways which cannot be said to be unimportant. Indeed the question arises whether Canon A.5 does not assert one standard of doctrine and the ASB inculcate another. Let us consider some cases in point.

I *The creed*

The origin of the creed lies in the formulation of the Christian confession which those who seek to enter the Church by baptism are required to make. There are innumerable examples of such credal formulations in the New Testament. These creeds assumed a trinitarian form in the second and third centuries. In the fourth and fifth centuries they received in successive councils increasingly precise definition in order to exclude error that was destructive of Catholic tradition. Thus the creed formulated at the Council of Nicaea in 325, and re-affirmed in an expanded form at Chalcedon in 451, became the baptismal creed in East and West for centuries, and is still recited universally in the eucharist. In the West, however, it was eventually replaced in baptism by the Apostles' Creed. This creed has now, however, been abandoned in the ASB rite of baptism. By what stages, then, has this fundamental doctrinal change been accomplished?

The creed anciently formed the syllabus of instruction for those who were being prepared during Lent for baptism at the Easter vigil. When the morning of Holy Saturday was reached they were required to repeat the creed which had thus been delivered to them. Later, at the vigil, they received the threefold baptism upon the confession of an abbreviated form of the creed. For example, the credal interrogations at Rome in the eighth century were:

> Dost thou believe in God the Father almighty? I believe.
>
> And dost thou believe in Jesus Christ his only Son our Lord, who was born and suffered? I believe.
>
> And dost thou believe in the Holy Spirit, the holy Church, the remission of sins, the resurrection of the flesh? I believe.[4]

---

4. *Liber Sacramentorum Romanae Aeclesiae Ordinis Amni Circuli* (Cod. Vat. Reg. lat. 316), ed L. C. Mohlberg, Roma, 1960, § 449.

It will be noticed that this baptismal formula, abbreviated though it is, retains specific, and not generalised, articles of faith. This use of the creed continued throughout the later middle ages, and accordingly in the Sarum rite (for example) the Apostles' Creed was recited by the Godparents at the conclusion of the catechumenate rites in the church porch, while the credal interrogations in an abbreviated form immediately preceded baptism.

This same pattern was followed in the 1549 Prayer Book. The recitation of the Apostles' Creed concluded the catechumenate rites in the church porch; but the credal interrogations before baptism were now in terms of the Apostles' Creed in full in question form. This repetition of the Apostles' Creed was avoided in 1552 by the virtual suppression of the catechumenate rites in the church porch. The Apostles' Creed was retained immediately before baptism, but now in the form of a single, not threefold, interrogation. These 1552 arrangements were followed in 1662. 1928 differed only in replacing the interrogatory form of the Apostles' Creed by the declaratory.

The Liturgical Commission's Report *Baptism and Confirmation* in 1958 introduced notable changes. In the normative order of the baptism and confirmation of those who are of age to answer for themselves, there was a return to the 1549 arrangement of the Apostles' Creed in threefold question form. But in the order of infant baptism, the Apostles' Creed was dropped, and in its place there was introduced a drastically simplified credal interrogation in the form of a single question:

> 'Do you believe in God the Father, who made you and all the world; and in his Son Jesus Christ, who redeemed you and all mankind; and in the Holy Ghost, who sanctifies you and all the elect people of God?'[5]

This form, the Commission explained, 'for pastoral reasons has been thought more suitable for godparents at Infant Baptism and for children making the Promises at Confirmation'.[6] The implications of this view were not spelt out, but they seem to include a low view both of the competence of Godparents at infant baptism and of the instruction given to children before Confirmation. The source of this simplified creed lay in the 1549 catechism, where it is offered as a summary of what

5. *Report,* SPCK 1959, p. 28; and again in Confirmation, p. 41.
6. ib., p. xi.

is to be 'chiefly learned' in the Apostles' Creed. It is to be observed that it is couched in general, and not specific, terms, the exact opposite of the credal interrogations before baptism in the Sarum rite.

Starting from a further Report on Baptism and Confirmation in 1967, a modified version of this general credal statement finally ousted the Apostles' Creed, and has prevailed in all its offspring — Series 2, Series 3, and ASB. It was modified in two ways. First, the verb 'to believe' was now correlated with the verb 'to trust': 'Do you believe and trust in God the Father' and so forth. Now while trust is one of the many nuances of meaning in belief, it is not clear why it has thus been singled out. Is there something lacking in the concept 'I believe'? Why should it now be thought necessary to supplement 'I believe' after nearly two thousand years in which this verb has been held to epitomise conversion? Neither in the New Testament nor in the various formulations of the Creed in the age of 'the ancient Fathers and Councils of the Church' has this particular pair of correlatives been used. Why should the Church of England now devalue the linguistic currency?

Secondly, in the case of the Holy Spirit the definite article has been replaced by the possessive pronoun: 'Do you believe and trust in *his* Holy Spirit?' Whose? The last proper noun to be used is 'Jesus Christ'. *His* Holy Spirit? But parallelism would suggest the Spirit of the Father: 'his Son', 'his Holy Spirit'. Both constructions can be illustrated from the New Testament: but the ambiguity remains. Yet a more serious objection lies in the introduction of the possessive pronoun where the Apostles' and Nicene Creeds have the definite article. This is to 'confuse the Persons'. The Catholic truth above all other is that in the Godhead there is a trinity of Persons and unity of substance. The Apostles' and Nicene Creeds bear witness to this truth. The ASB baptismal creed muffs it. On this point tradition is set aside by the adoption of a new and ill-conceived formula.[7]

But we have not yet reached the most serious defects of the ASB baptismal formula. We have already noticed that the formula is couched in general and not specific terms. Thus Christ is said to have redeemed mankind. But nothing is said of his incarnation, passion and resurrection, which are of essential importance to the Christian faith. It is in consequence now possible, and has been possible since the introduction of Series 2 baptism, to enter the Church without confessing these

7. It should be noticed that in 'A celebration of faith to welcome Pope John Paul II on the eve of Pentecost', held at Canterbury on May 29, 1982, the definite article replaced the possessive pronoun. Was this done in deference to the credal convictions of the Pope?

basic Christological truths. Are they deemed to be 'unsuitable' for Godparents at infant baptism, and not only for children but also for adults, after instruction, at confirmation? Why, then, should the concept of 'redemption' be thought more 'suitable'? Is this easier for Godparents and everybody else to understand? In the same way a wholly generalised statement is made about the Holy Spirit, and nothing is said about the Church, the remission of sins, and resurrection. These doctrines can hardly be said to be anything but central to Christianity.

Finally, these generalised statements fall short of what the Church believes. Thus the ASB baptismal creed says of God the Father that he 'made the world'; but the Catholic creeds say 'heaven and earth'. The ASB creed says of Christ that he 'redeemed mankind'; but the Catholic creeds give precision to the meaning of redemption. The ASB creed says that the Holy Spirit 'gives life to the people of God'; but the Nicene Creed says 'the Lord, the giver of life'. This reduced ASB creed is said, by the bishop, to be 'the faith of the Church'. This is a misleading statement. It is at best a bowdlerised form of the faith of the Church.[8]

The baptismal creed is of primordial significance. An undisputed Western formula lies ready to hand in the Apostles' Creed, which hitherto in the BCP has formed an integral part of Anglican inheritance. In an age of ecumenical endeavour every consideration should lead us to make the most of what we have in common. It is then deplorable that in ASB baptism a novel and reduced credal formulation should be adopted.

II *The baptismal liturgy*

But this is not the only doctrinal flaw in ASB baptism. Three others must be mentioned. First, the form of renunciation; secondly, the prayer at the font; and thirdly, the relationship of baptism and confirmation.

The renunciation, first, appears under the curious heading 'The Decision'. (But does not 'I believe' also involve a decision?) It includes three questions. The first is: 'Do you turn to Christ?' It is otiose. Turning to Christ is what renunciation and belief together express, but with sharper definition. It lacks precedent. But this is not a consideration that weighs very heavily with the Church of England in its present mood.

8. It should again be noticed that in the Canterbury celebration of faith, while the ASB questions were put by the Archbishop, the Pope, and the Moderator of the Free Church Federal Council in turn, the congregation responded with the words of the Apostles' Creed. The Pope, the Archbishop and the Moderator could justifiably claim that this was the faith of the Church. The alteration in the ASB text was a tacit acknowledgement that something is the matter with the ASB creed.

The second question is: 'Do you repent of your sins?' This involves an unusual use of the verb 'to repent'. This verb is used thirty-four times in the New Testament. Luke once uses it with *apo*, 'from', sc. 'from wickedness' (Ac. 8:22). The Seer uses it five times (out of twelve) with *ek*, 'from', sc. from fornication, murder, etc. (Revn. 2:21f, 9:20f, 16:11). But in all other cases in the New Testament the verb 'to repent' is used absolutely, and means 'to change one's mind' or 'to convert'. In the context of the baptismal promises it is both renunciation and belief together which constitute repentance, and which entail a total change or re-orientation of mind. 'Repent' is the first word of Christ in his proclamation of the Kingdom. Hence to restrict repentance to 'sins' is once again to devalue the linguistic currency.

The third question, 'Do you renounce evil?', is not the least unsatisfactory. It is indeed the only question involving renunciation. But what is renounced is an abstraction, 'evil'. This must be compared with the Christian tradition as a whole. The renunciation of Satan, or the Devil, and all his angels, his pomps, and his works, is in all rites, Eastern and Western, the starting point of the baptismal liturgy. It might even be said that this feature is the most consistent and stable element in all rites. It survives with considerable force in the BCP. How then has it come to be abandoned in the ASB? Perhaps it is thought 'appropriate' to demythologise Satan. But we are on a slippery slope here. Demythologise Satan, and what happens to the angels and archangels at the beginning of the eucharistic prayer? Moreover, there is a dynamic character about evil, which passes unrecognised in the use of a purely abstract concept. Every rational person is against evil, as he is against sin. But merely to renounce 'evil' is to mask the insidious forces that men and women are up against. The debate about demythologisation in the recent study of the New Testament has taught us that once 'myth' is understood, it has to be re-employed. A vocabulary drawn from the modern secular world is inadequate to express Christian belief in all its depth. Symbolic language is indispensable. In the renunciation, then, as in the profession of faith the ASB falls short of the BCP.

Secondly, the next doctrinal flaw in ASB baptism lies in the blessing of the font. In order to appreciate this, we need to understand the background. The blessing of water for baptism is a feature of all baptismal liturgies, Eastern and Western, from antiquity. In the first English Prayer Book of 1549 there was accordingly an order for blessing the font which included (a) the actual blessing of the water, (b) short acts of prayer and (c) a longer prayer for those about to be baptised. The blessing of the water ran as follows: 'Send down, we beseech thee, the same thy Holy Spirit to assist us, and to be present at this our invocation of thy holy Name: Sanctify + this fountain of baptism, thou that art the sanctifier of all things, that by the power of thy word all those that shall be baptised therein may be spiritually regenerated, and made the children of everlasting adoption'. But this prayer was abandoned in 1552, and thus there remained only the (reduced) petitions and the prayer for the baptised. However in 1662, although the 1549 blessing of the water was not restored, a blessing formula was introduced into the prayer for the baptised: 'Sanctify this water to the mystical washing away of sin: and grant that this child now to be baptised therein may receive the fulness of thy grace', and so forth. Thus in 1662 the sanctification of the water was deemed to be efficacious in the washing away of sin.

What has happened in the ASB? The words 'Bless this water' certainly occur; but in the purpose clause that follows the cleansing from sin appears to be referred to the future, 'that your servants who are washed in it may be made one with Christ in his death and resurrection, *to be cleansed* and delivered from all sin'. Furthermore, the invocation of the Holy Spirit refers not to the water, as in 1549 and in all Catholic rites, but to those who are to be baptised, with a view to bringing them to new birth in the future: 'Send your Holy Spirit upon them to bring them to new birth in the family of your Church, and raise them with Christ to full and eternal life'. Any suggestion of baptismal regeneration here, so strongly marked a feature in the 1662 rite, seems to be studiously avoided.

Finally, the question of the gift of the Holy Spirit in baptism and confirmation, the subject of so much controversy in the past, is inescapable. So long as baptism and confirmation constituted a unified initiation rite, performed at the Easter vigil, in the presence of the bishop, the grounds for controversy did not exist. It was only with the gradual dismemberment of the rite in the later middle ages in the West that problems arose. The Sarum rite more or less perpetuated the old Roman rite, but distributed its parts into different times and places. Catechumenate rites took place at the church door, followed by baptism at the font; confirmation followed when the bishop was in the neighbourhood; and Holy Communion was to be given after baptism 'si aetas eius id deposcat'. The Holy Spirit was the agent in baptism, and the sevenfold gifts of the Holy Spirit were given in confirmation. The 1549 rite of baptism introduced a petition for the gift of the Holy Spirit at the conclusion of the catechumenate rites at the church door, without referring this gift either to baptism or to confirmation in particular. The

1549 rite of cofirmation continued the old prayer for the sevenfold gifts of the Holy Spirit: 'Send down from heaven, we beseech thee, O Lord, upon them thy (sic) Holy Ghost the Comforter, with the manifold gifts of grace', and so forth.

A major doctrinal change, however, was made in 1552. The catechumenate rites at the church door were suppressed, and the concluding prayer for the gift of the Holy Spirit was transferred to the immediate context of baptism at the font. Accordingly the prayer for the sevenfold gifts of the Holy Spirit specifically in confirmation was modified, and now read: '*Strengthen* them, we beseech thee, O Lord, with the Holy Ghost the Comforter, and daily increase in them thy manifold gifts of grace'. This remained the standpoint of 1662.

The 1958 report *Baptism and Confirmation* marked a fresh development by returning to the unified rite of baptism, confirmation and the eucharist as the normative form of initiation. In consequence it was possible to return to the early medieval and 1549 theology of initiation in which the Holy Spirit is the agent in baptism, and the sevenfold gifts of the Holy Spirit are bestowed in confirmation. The confirmation prayer embodying this petition in 1958 was virtually the same as the confirmation prayer in 1549. But a new formula was devised for the imposition of the hand, which was obscure to the point of meaninglessness: 'Confirm, O Lord, thy servant N with thy Holy Spirit. . .'.[9] This 1958 report was, however, sidetracked, and it was not until 1967 that Series 2 Baptism and Confirmation, more or less on these lines, appeared. Series 3 Initiation Services were again delayed until the Ely Report of 1971, *Christian Initiation: Birth and Growth in the Christian Society*, had been published and debated.

This report was founded upon the controversial view that baptism in water in the name of the Holy Trinity is the whole of Christian initiation, and cannot be added to, supplemented or completed. Confirmation was therefore invested with a novel significance, namely, that of commissioning and commitment. This view of baptism and confirmation did not eventually commend itself to the General Synod. But meantime the Liturgical Commission had prepared Series 3 rites of baptism and confirmation which went a long way towards adopting the views of the Ely Commission. These Series 3 rites have since been incorporated into ASB. Thus in the collect (§4), the bishop's exhortation

---

9. This formula has been retained in Series 2 and 3 and the ASB. An unconvincing defence of it is put forward in the 1958 report (pp. xiif.).

(§12), and the blessing of the font (§17), fresh emphasis is placed upon the association of the Holy Spirit with baptism in such a way as to suggest that baptism is indeed, as the Ely Commission maintained, 'the one and complete act of Christian initiation'.[10] The petition, for example, 'Send your Holy Spirit upon them', has been taken from the confirmation prayer in 1549, 1958 and Series 2, and transferred to the blessing of the font.

To sum up this discussion of the baptismal liturgy, while the 1958 report looked to the early, medieval and 1549 rites of baptism and confirmation, the ASB looks to 1552 and indeed intensifies its theology by frankly investing baptism alone with all the properties of the whole complex rite of Christian initiation.

If we also bear in mind the treatment of the renunciations and the Creed in ASB baptism, we are driven to conclude that the ASB baptismal liturgy has moved theologically away from the BCP and a long way from the teaching of the Fathers and Councils of the Church.

III *The eucharistic liturgy*

The Church of England prides itself on being the Church of the land, and not an eponymous Church. Anglicans do not regard themselves as being of Cranmer, as others are of Luther or Calvin or Wesley. Nevertheless Cranmer's theological opinions have nowhere more deeply impressed themselves on the Church of England than in the eucharistic liturgy — if we may use an expression of our time, not his. He embodied these opinions in an essay which forms an invaluable commentary on the communion rites of the 1549 and 1552 Prayer Books, *A defence of the true and catholic doctrine of the sacrament of the Body and Blood of our Saviour Jesus Christ.*[11]

In the Preface to the 1580 edition of this work, which is said to have had the benefit of his last revision, Cranmer described as the two chief roots of popery 'the popish doctrine of transubstantiation, of the real presence of Christ's flesh and blood in the sacrament of the altar, (as they call it); and of the sacrifice and oblation of Christ made by the priest for the salvation of the quick and the dead'.[12] In order to pull up these roots, Cranmer in 1549 abandoned the Roman Canon of the Mass, i.e. all that

---

10. *Christian Initiation: Birth and Growth in the Christian Society*, CIO, 1971, paras. 67-69.
11. Crammer's *Defence*, ed. C.H.H.Wright, London 1907; differently arranged for the Parker Society, ed. J. E. Cox, Cambridge 1844.
12. op. cit., ed. Wright, p. xxiv.

follows the sanctus and benedictus, and replaced it with a new, long and complex prayer in three parts: the first part gathered together the petitions from the canon, and is now familiar to us as the 'prayer for the Church militant'; the second part contained the memorial of the last supper, and is now familiar to us as the 1662 'Prayer of Consecration'; and the third part consisted of the remembrance of Christ's passion, resurrection and ascension, together with the offering of ourselves, our souls and bodies, again familiar to us as the so-called prayer of oblation. Cranmer's rejection of the doctrine of transubstantiation and of the real presence was signalled by the rubric ordering that the dominical words should be said 'without any elevation or showing the sacrament to the people'. And his rejection of 'the sacrifice and oblation of Christ made by the priest' was made evident in his abandonment of the oblation formula in the Roman canon, namely, 'we offer unto thy glorious majesty, of thine own gifts and bounty . . . the holy bread of eternal life and the cup of everlasting salvation', and the substitution of a new formula, namely, 'we . . . do celebrate and make here before thy divine majesty, *with* these thy holy gifts, the memorial which thy Son hath willed us to make: having in remembrance his blessed passion', and so forth. What was now to be offered was not the bread and cup, but ourselves, our souls and bodies.

This re-writing of the eucharistic prayer — again to use a modern expression, not Cranmer's — was too subtle for some and not plain enough by half. 'Mistakers' like Gardiner sought to gloss it in terms of the traditional canon. Cranmer therefore returned to the drawing board. 1552 made 1549 fully perfect. The three parts of the complex prayer with which Cranmer replaced the Roman canon were now split up. Cranmer's Order of the Communion of 1548, originally designed for use with the Latin mass, after the canon, became the matrix of the memorial of the last supper. Communion followed the narrative of the supper. The so-called prayer of oblation, i.e. of ourselves, our souls and bodies, followed communion, as an alternative to the prayer of thanksgiving. The 1549 petition, 'Bless and sanctify these thy gifts and creatures of bread and wine', like the sanctification of the water at baptism in 1549, was dropped. Instead there was substituted a new petition, 'Grant that we, receiving these thy creatures of bread and wine . . . in remembrance of his death and passion, may be partakers of his most blessed body and blood'. The manual acts in the narrative of the last supper were also dropped. A new communion formula was introduced, namely, 'Take and eat this in remembrance that Christ died for thee, and feed on him in thy heart by faith, with thanksgiving'. It epitomised the whole rite, which was now nothing more nor less than a communion service in remembrance of Christ's passion.

The Caroline revisers of 1662 went some way towards modifying this rite. A simple offertory was restored. The memorial prayer was now called 'the Prayer of Consecration', and detailed manual acts were reintroduced in the course of the narrative of the institution. The 1549 formula for the administration of Holy Communion, 'The body of our Lord Jesus Christ. . .', had already been united with the 1552 formula in 1559, and this combined formula was now retained. The revisers of 1662 thus restored to the bread and wine in the communion service, as to the water of the font in baptism, the concept of consecration or sanctification.

The appearance of the Book of Common Prayer in 1549, and of the Tridentine Missale Romanum in 1570, was followed by centuries of unparalleled rigidity of rites. The standardisation of texts was made possible by printing, and the new concepts of authority in Church and state resulted in the enforcement of standards. In the course of time, however, the volume of liturgical knowledge grew steadily, a fresh appreciation of traditional texts was developed, and the systematic presentation of the history of liturgy gradually became possible. The liturgical controversies of the later middle ages and sixteenth century necessarily came to be seen in a changed light. Cranmer's rejection of liturgical tradition, and of the Roman canon in particular, in favour of a doctrinal *idea* expressed in newly composed prayers, could not escape re-assessment.

The two chief roots of error were in his view the doctrine of transubstantiation and the papistical priests making their mass a sacrifice propitiatory.[13] But were his protests correctly targeted? The doctrine of transubstantiation was developed in order to deepen the understanding of the eucharistic mystery. But its categories were not indigenous to the traditional language of liturgy, and the Latin rite had indeed served the Western Church for a millenium before the doctrine came to be formulated, accepted, and imposed with authority. As for the question of sacrifice, however this was understood in the late middle ages, the Roman canon specifically unites the clergy and the people in the offering of sacrifice: nos servi tui sed et plebs tua sancta . . . offerimus praeclarae maiestati tuae de tuis donis ac datis panem sanctum vitae aeternae et calicem salutis perpetuae.

13. ib., p. 232.

Anglicans need carefully to weigh this question in view of their appeal in matters of doctrine not only to Holy Scripture but also to the ancient Fathers and Councils of the Church. The Roman canon at least in its central paragraphs emerged in the fourth century, and its text and doctrine would have been familiar to the Latin Fathers of that time, including Ambrose and Augustine, and to the representatives of the Roman Church at the Council of Chalcedon in 451. Moreover, the doctrine of the eucharist was not in dispute between East and West. Thus the doctrine and language of the Roman canon were fully congruous with the doctrine and language of those Greek anaphoral prayers familiar to the Greek Fathers of the age and the Greek representatives at the ecumenical councils of the fourth and fifth centuries. Thus Cranmer's rejection of the Roman canon places him at odds with the ancient Fathers and Councils of the Church, and the doctrinal *idea* enshrined by him in the 1549 and 1552 Prayer Books would have seemed strange indeed to them.

Of course, in defence of Cranmer it might be urged that on this question of eucharistic doctrine and practice the ancient Fathers and Councils of the Church were mistaken, and had misunderstood Holy Scripture, and that the appeal of the Church of England now is only to *such* teachings of the Fathers and Councils as are agreeable to the said Scriptures. Apologists proceeding on these lines would have a difficult task on their hands, not least because *The Apostolic Tradition* witnesses essentially to this doctrinal tradition in the early part of the third century, which takes us a long way back towards the period of the New Testament. Did eucharistic doctrine and practice go fundamentally wrong in the course of the second century? Or did the early Church understand these matters better than our reformers?

The elements that are central to the eucharistic prayer are four: the *traditio* of the institution of the eucharist, *anamnesis*, *oblatio*, and *invocatio* or *epiclesis*. They do not however follow one another as separate and distinct items, but cohere in a single integrated whole. The sacred *traditio* of the supper and the dominical words is constituted by sacrificial language.[14] In the Gospels it serves to interpret the meaning of the Lord's death, while in the liturgies it determines the character of the rite. The *oblatio* offers the sacrifice to the Father. In Eastern rites the language of sacrifice is used; in the Roman rite, the language of the supper

---

14. See J. Jeremias, *The eucharistic words of Jesus,* ET 2nd ed. SCM 1964, pp. 218ff.

tradition. Who offers? In the first place, Christ. But secondarily the Church, in virtue of a double title — his union of our human nature with his divine nature in the incarnation, and our baptismal union with him. What is offered? In the first place, Χριστος ἐσταυρωμἐυος, Christ crucified; secondarily, the Church itself as baptised into his death. Next, the point of the *anamnesis*, which is almost always placed in a participial construction, is to define the intention with which the sacrifice is offered. The death, resurrection and parousia differentiate the Church's sacrifice from any other sacrifice, Jewish or pagan. Finally, there is the *invocatio* or *epiclesis*, the purpose of which is to unite the Church's temporal sacrifice with the eternal sacrifice of Christ. The Roman *invocatio* thinks of the taking of the Church's gifts by the holy Angel — probably Christ himself — to the heavenly altar. The Eastern *epiclesis* thinks of the illapse of the Holy Spirit upon the bread and cup to make or show them to be the body and blood of Christ. These four elements, variously distributed in different liturgical families, constitute the essence of the eucharistic prayer in a unified ritual act.

In rejecting the doctrine of the sacrifice of the Mass, Cranmer, though he could scarcely have known it, was rejecting the universal eucharistic doctrine of Christian antiquity and the consensus of Eastern and Western liturgies. We must now ask, in the light of this discussion, what the consequences are in the ASB of recent attempts to reconstruct the eucharistic prayer in the Church of England. It will clarify matters if we analyse the ASB eucharistic prayers in terms of these same four elements. Seven prayers are involved: five in Rite A numbered 1 to 4, together with the modern language version of the BCP prayer of consecration (no longer however so called); and two in Rite B, numbered 1 and 2. A1, 2, and 4 are derived from old Series 3, 2 and 1. A3 is related superficially to Prex Eucharistica II in the Missale Romanum of 1970. B1 and 2 are derived from old Series 1 and 2.

In regard, first, to the sacred *traditio* of the last supper B1 and 2 and BCP(A) all retain the manual acts of 1662; and indeed B1 and 2 retain the BCP title 'the Prayer of Consecration'. An intention therefore to consecrate the bread and the wine is evidently present. By contrast A1, 2, 3 and 4 all abandon manual acts as an integral part of the text. A prefatory note indeed allows the use of 'traditional manual acts'. It must however follow from the dethronement of the manual acts in the body of the text that the understanding of consecration by the dominical words in Rite A 1 to 4, though not denied, has been tacitly abandoned. Thus there is formally a return to the prayer in the 1552 book. By contrast, it should be noticed that the concept of consecration by the dominical words has been continued in the new Roman Missal, both in the text and also in the commentary, the *Institutio generalis*.

Secondly, the *anamnesis* of Christ's death and resurrection has been introduced into A1 to 4 and B1 and 2 — we might say re-introduced from 1549. Since the *anamnesis* forms an invariable element in all eucharistic prayers from antiquity, this looks like a solid gain, until the question of what has been gained is asked. As we have already seen, the purpose of the *anamnesis* is to define the ends for which the sacrifice is offered, and thus the *anamnesis* must lead on precisely to the offering of the sacrifice.

But here thirdly, when it should come to *oblatio*, different voices are heard. One point can be cleared up straightaway. Old Series 2 and 3 prayers — A1 and 2 and B 2 — all reject the offering of the bread and cup. This results from the failure of such an offering formula in draft Series 2 to secure a sufficient majority in the House of Laity, although it had the overwhelming approval of both Houses of the Convocations, in 1967.[15] Thereafter the Series 2 and 3 type of prayer included the 1549 formula 'to make a memorial *with* the bread and cup' — the very formula, that is to say, with which Cranmer repudiated the oblation formula in the Roman Canon.

The Series 1 type of prayer — A4 and B1 — represents a different case. In old Series 1, reuniting the prayer of oblation to the prayer of consecration, God is asked to accept 'this our sacrifice of praise and thanksgiving'. This expression , in this context, can be understood in conformity with the Romano-Byzantine tradition, since what God is asked to accept must be offered. *Sacrificium laudis* is a term used in the Roman canon for the eucharistic oblation, at least in the Memento paragraph and in some (earlier) super oblata prayers.[16] This

15. *The Liturgical Conference 1967: Report of Proceedings* Tuesday, April 25, 1967. CIO. 'The Chairman: I put question 2: Would the Conference agree to 'We offer unto thee' as the only form of words . . . *The question was carried by an overwhelming majority in the Convocations and, in the House of Laity, by 101 in favour and 86 against.' (p 36).* Subsequently Canon R.D.C. Jasper moved an amendment in the following form: 'Wherefore, O Lord, with this bread and this cup, we make the memorial of his saving passion, his resurrection from the dead and his glorious ascension into heaven, and we look for the coming of his kingdom. We pray thee to accept this our duty and service.' He added: 'That is not ideal. I am under no delusions about that. I am merely putting it out as a possible stopgap solution which might tide us over until we can think this thing out in peace and quiet' (pp 37f). No vote appears to have been taken, except to adjourn the discussion. The following day, at a joint synod of the Convocations, a motion embodying this amendment 'was put separately to both Houses of each Convocation and carried unanimously in the Upper Houses and by substantial majorities in the Lower Houses' (The Chronicle of Convocation, no 2, 1967, April, p 115). So much for the ancient Fathers and Councils.

16. *Sacrificium laudis* does not occur after the *traditio* of the institution of the eucharist. The late Dr G. G. Willis drew a distinction in the Roman rite between the offering of the unconsecrated gifts and the offering of the consecrated gifts. *Sacrificium laudis* is used only of the former, not of the latter.

interpretation was given explicit support in the revised version of A4 (GS 364A), for this at first read 'we offer you this sacrifice of praise and thanksgiving'. However, in the final debate the text was interpolated so as to read, 'we offer you *through him* this sacrifice of praise and thanksgiving'. This interpolation effectively imposed a different meaning on the sentence, namely, the offering to God of a sacrifice that consists of our praise and thanksgiving, and not the offering to God of the sacrifice that uniquely gives him praise, that is to say, the Church's sacrifice *de tuis donis ac datis*.

Finally, under the heading of *oblatio*, we must consider the wording of A3: 'we bring before you this bread and this cup'. A3, as we have noticed, bears some relationship to Prex Eucharistica II in the Missale Romanum. But this prayer in the anamnesis-oblation paragraph reads, 'we offer to you the bread of life and the cup of everlasting salvation'. This of course is essentially the formula in draft Series 2 which failed to command a sufficient majority in the House of Laity in 1967. The wording, therefore, 'we bring before you', instead of 'we offer', shows how intolerant the Church of England is of this characteristically catholic formula. For 'we offer' is catholic in the sense of satisfying the Vincentian Canon *quod ubique, quod semper, quod ab omnibus*, since it was in all eucharistic rites without exception until the sixteenth century reformations. It must be left to others to judge what 'bring before' really means. But it is painful, weakening and confusing to have at the heart of the eucharistic prayer such obfuscation.

The last element in the eucharist prayer to be considered is the *invocatio* or *epiclesis*. There is of course nothing in the ASB prayers to correspond with the Latin invocatio, that is, the thought of bringing the church's oblation to the heavenly altar. But the epiclesis is another matter. The phrase 'the power of the Holy Spirit' occurs everywhere these days, even in the modern language version of the Nicene Creed. It is used in A1 to 4 (twice in A3) and B1 and 2. The epiclesis is Eastern in origin, and is of extreme antiquity. In all Eastern liturgies it is used in the form of asking God to send down the Holy Spirit to fill the sacrifice which the Church offers, and to make and consecrate the bread and cup so that they become the body and blood of Christ. In addition the Holy Spirit is in some rites invoked upon those who offer and receive the eucharist. In the ASB prayers it is only this latter idea which receives unambiguous expression. 'The power of the Holy Spirit' is invoked only in a virtual sense, with the intention that the gifts of bread and wine 'may be to us' (not 'become') the body and blood of Christ. This limitation, without parallel in Eastern, and now modern Roman, eucharistic prayers, is of course fully consistent with the exclusion, already noticed, of the eucharistic oblation.

The four elements of *traditio, anamnesis, oblatio*, and *invocatio* or *epiclesis* cohere in a single cultic act. If, as in the ASB, following 1549 and 1552, the eucharistic oblation is excluded, everything else falls apart. Thus in the ASB there is traditio without consecration, anamnesis without offering, and epiclesis without change in the gifts.

It has been said that there is no mind in the ASB. Since the 1958 Baptism and Confirmation report and draft Holy Communion Series 2, political forces have taken over the work of revision. In the process there has been a return to 1549 and 1552, and the doctrinal position of the reformers has been secured. The modest revisions in 1662 have been dismantled, and not one single point of Catholic doctrine has been gained. The treatment of the baptismal creed is indicative of the whole tendency of ASB. There has been a doctrinal retreat on a wide front from the teaching of the ancient Fathers and Councils of the Church. To what traditions in that formative age of the Church does the Church of England now unambiguously and unreservedly appeal?

Michael Moreton is lecturer in theology at the University of Exeter, and rector of St Mary Steps, Exeter.

5
A ministry of service

Peter Moore

So glorious let thy pastors shine,
That by their speaking oves the world may learn — John Keble, This Christian Year, St. John Baptist.

Barchester Towers is a classic description of the Church of England in the nineteenth century. It paints a picture of a world within a world: of an ecclesiastical society largely independent of the secular with a highly formalised hierarchy supported by independent | financial resources and inherited privilege. As such it affords a striking contrast to the picture of the twentieth century church, struggling against heavy odds to be more closely identified with the world it serves. That service is its ministry, and it is with this ministry, lay as well as clerical, that this essay is concerned. My object is to reveal not only its strengths but also its weaknesses. I believe passionately in the ministry of the Church and long to see it strengthened and, where necessary, reformed.

That there is a general dis-ease cannot be denied. The Guardian last year printed an article about the Church of England entitled 'The End is Nigh' and the Daily Telegraph a leader about the Church headed 'Bottoming Out' (March 1983). The same paper in December 1982 had printed an article by a Fellow of an Oxford College 'When Priests No Longer Believe in What They Preach' and in the same month a series under the heading 'Bishops in a Sea of Troubles Which Surround the Eighties', in which Graham Turner's investigation about how Bishops live revealed a very different picture from that drawn by Trollope. Although the truth may be somewhere between these two extremes, it is clear that many questions are being asked about the Christian ministry today, and a variety of answers offered. No longer does the Church of England speak with a single voice. Yet Ministry, and the proper understanding of it, is basic to all church life. For if on the one hand it is equated with service, it is also on the other the agency or representation of a superior. A Christian minister is a servant of the servants of God, and his or her pattern is Jesus Christ, who is the touchstone by which ministry is to be judged. How does it measure up now?

One classic Anglican work is *A Priest to the Temple* by George Herbert. Although it is specifically clerical and breathes a rural pre-industrial revolution air, it distils many truths. The opening sentence reads 'A Pastor is the deputy of Christ, for reducing of many to the obedience of God'; and speaking of the priesthood generally Herbert wrote of 'the dignity, in that a priest may do that which Christ did, and by His authority and as His viceregent; the duty, in that a priest is to do that which Christ did, and after His manner, both for doctrine and life.'

Ministry may be perceived as holiness, as service, as sacrament and as obedience; in these contexts criticisms, though general, do not apply to everyone. But the worldliness of Barchester still survives, in a different form. Too often the church goes with the world and fails to proclaim the uncomfortable standards of Christ.

Ministry as Holiness

'The things of God for the people of God.' This sentence appears in the Orthodox Liturgy before the communion of the people, and the Greek words connote holy things for holy people. We, the people of God, Christ's church, are all called to holiness, to be distinct and in some measure apart. This is not something special for the clergy — nor is it, unfortunately, particularly characteristic of them. Yet those called to leadership are also called to a particularity of holiness. Much depends upon our definition of this specific Christian quality. George Herbert however makes it quite clear. It is that personal fellowship with God that the transfiguration symbolises in the Gospel record; something which irradiates a person; the reason why Moses veiled his face after meeting the Lord God on Sinai.

The artist may represent it by a halo, and to the ordinary man and woman it is that indefinable but unavoidable impression of other-worldliness conveyed by some rare souls — lay and ordained. It is something for which the laity are right to look in their clergy, a mediation of the things of God which transfigures the human with the light of Christ. It should also be a characteristic of all men, women, and children; the evidence of the fact recalled by St Peter that we are 'a chosen race, a royal priesthood, a holy nation, God's own people'. Herbert wrote of this too:

> All may of thee partake;
> Nothing can be so mean,
> Which with this tincture, 'for thy sake',
> Will not grow bright and clean.

Herbert stands out just because his life witnessed to the things of which he wrote. Indeed the church has nurtured an unbroken succession of saints. This tradition of personal holiness is a characteristic of ministry which has never entirely disappeared, though at times it may have run a secret course. It was characteristic of the Tractarians. Keble, Pusey and Newman spring to mind, and more recently Edward King, the saintly Bishop of Lincoln. It was characteristic of 19th-century evangelicals like William Wilberforce and Charles Simeon.

Holiness needs to be reclaimed as typical of contemporary church life. But it is always a secondary, derivative quality. It is not, like social conscience or political involvement, either obvious to outsiders, or even welcome. But it shines through the darkness of prison camps and mental hospitals, and through persecution on a world-wide scale; we must look for it in vicarage and bishop's palace as well as in diocesan office, and factory. Shine it must, and will, where individuals are friends of God who find time for his presence and so find his presence in their time. It is not only the country parson's library which is a holy life (Herbert).

In an age obsessed with saving time, Christians are right to ask for what purpose, and to what use, the time saved is put. Conversely, we are daily inundated with an avalanche of paper in reports and consultative documents and agendas and minutes which consume the world's forests at an alarming rate and do little to forward its salvation. Disciples of Christ, whether lay or ordained, must by definition be people who find time to be with Christ. Human friendships either grow or wither. They seldom remain unchanged — change is a condition of life and nature knows no standing still; there is either growth or decay.

The same is true of the spiritual life. It is not talking about a Person (of which there is far too much) or reading about a Person (of which there is too little) but living with a Person, and that needs time. Time is the context in which we prepare for eternity and no one can escape the challenge. Are we ready to make time? Do you honestly make time for God? Are we concerned rather with the organisation and bureaucracy of the Church than with God himself? These are discomforting questions which we cannot avoid. What do they say to the vast and expensive structures which, both centrally and in the diocese, we have allowed to luxuriate? The synodical system, hailed by some as a means of liberating the church, has in fact done nothing of the sort. Rather it has multiplied time-wasting meetings and confused democracy with church order. Of course the pressures of twentieth century life are vastly different from those our forefathers knew. But without holiness there can be only the shadow of discipleship, not its reality. Is this obvious from the timetables of theological colleges, the agendas of church meetings, and the lives of the holy common people of God — led by the example of their priests? If not, and I suspect the honest answer is in the negative, then we must return and renew our assault upon the mountain of personal transfiguration, whatever may be the cost.

Ministry as Service

Christ's lifestyle was one of service. His contemporaries found this hard to accept and it ended (or began) with crucifixion. The pages of the gospel depict a ministry different from that of Barchester, and although the epistle from the Ordinal of the Book of Common Prayer is about varieties of ministry, the gospel depicts the Good Shepherd as the pattern for them all. The Good Shepherd said 'I lay down my life for the sheep.' Mercifully few are called to do that. But we are all called to a life of service rather than one of domination. In practical terms this has meant, and still means, pastoral care for a parish. In this Anglicanism has a distinguished history.

But times and conditions have changed. No longer is there a priest in every parish, though everyone lives in a parish for which a priest is responsible. No longer can all the clergy hope to be in that close personal contact with their flock that was typical of the golden age of Anglicanism. Some indeed might say it only belongs to the fantasy of historians. Yet the Church of England retains, and for the most part tries to honour, a responsibility for those who have not contracted out of it. This responsibility remains and the great difference is the manner in which it is exercised through a variety of ministries, lay as well as ordained; whole-time as well as part-time; stipendiary and non-stipendiary. In some respects this pluriformity of ministries is in advance of its general acceptance by lay people, and we face an educational task if new (though actually primitive) methods are to find acceptance.

At the heart of it all there remains the fundamental responsibility of the parish priest for his people — a responsibility which cannot be wholly discharged at second or even third hand. This 'cure of souls' must entail a personal knowledge of the flock. Anglicans have an honourable tradition to uphold. The example of countless priests, not only George Herbert, witnesses to this, as does the sacrificial devotion of town clergy, particularly in the industrial squalor of the nineteenth century. But we cannot evade the question whether this tradition, changed as it must of necessity be, remains — or has it been totally or in large part submerged by an ecclesiastical bureaucracy which assumes that people know where to find a priest if they want one? It also presumes that people will go to a total stranger they may never have seen, let alone met.

Pastoral care means knowing people, not sending them forms to fill up. It means being sensitive to their needs and open to their hesitations and prejudices. House to house visiting is certainly out of fashion, though it may be observed in passing that because it is impractical in many places, it tends to be abandoned in all. So a new strand in the process of alienation is being developed — ignorance; ignorance not only of who the clergy and other ministers are and what they are really like, but ignorance of the church and what it stands for and is trying to achieve. Many read little, and there is a sense in which the church remains far too literate-orientated. TV, the greatest single influence of opinion, has little time for those who cannot pay — unless that deficiency can be made up for in terms of newsworthy scandal. The gap between 'us' and 'them' widens as the pews continue to empty. Even here there are signs of hope. Bold experiments are being made with groups and house churches and various forms of ministry. But the danger, not to say the tendency, remains that the supplementary becomes the staple, and the experiment the substitute for the normal.

Ministry as Sacrament

The Catechism defines a sacrament as 'an outward and visible sign of an inward and spiritual grace given unto us, ordained by Christ himself, as a means whereby we receive the same, and a pledge to assure us thereof.' Ordination is a sacrament, so those ordained themselves become living sacraments, signs of grace. Herein lies the awesomeness of Holy Orders. Feeble humans are signs of grace, and to emphasise this the Thirty-Nine Articles remind us that 'the Unworthiness of the Ministers . . . hinders not the effect of the Sacrament.' All this because Christ chose and sent apostles, giving them explicit charge to baptise and teach and reconcile people, not only to each other, but primarily to God.

The ministry is a given thing, Christ's pledge. It is not therefore something to be bartered in an ecumenical bazaar; nor is it something to be abandoned on a simplistic understanding of the prayer for unity. It is something to be used and treasured and enjoyed. We sometimes overlook his wish that our joy should be full! The Tractarians recalled the Church of England to a proper appreciation of the sacraments. They widened Anglican horizons which had been reduced by history and prejudice, and they recalled us to the sense of catholicity (universality) of the church. Anglicanism is only a part of the whole; but it *is* that, and has its place within a world-wide context. The Sacraments, fundamental to the Christian revelation and an extension of the doctrine of the Incarnation, are part of our inheritance, and in this sense Ministry and Tradition are two sides of one coin. Indeed the continuity of the church, exemplified by its sacraments, provides an unbroken chain of tradition reaching to Christ's commission to his apostles.

Part of this tradition is the maintenance of right faith — orthodoxy. Anglican teaching has stood upon these facts which are part of our common inheritance, and though they were overlooked at times, it was the saints and scholars, priests and prophets of the last century who restored them to their rightful position in the Church of England. They are, however, now being challenged again, and on a deeper level. The rumpus over Hensley Henson's nomination as Bishop of Durham, like that of his successor, at least shows a concern for right faith based upon the Creeds which belong to Christianity, not just to Anglicans. It would seem that liberalism invests heresy with a halo, and does so without challenge from the bishops who promised at their consecration 'to banish and drive away all erroneous and strange doctrine contrary to God's Word' — a promise significantly dropped in the Alternative Service Book. Furthermore a theological egalitarianism sees one ministry as no different from another, ordained or lay, apostolic or reformed, and therefore can plead with specious conviction for the utter novelty of lay celebration of the Holy Communion. On the other hand lies the rejection of tradition, a rejection which derives from the current rootlessness of secular society. There is a real danger that the church may only too successfully identify itself with the society its ministry is to redeem. If heresy is necessary to establish the truth, then there is plenty of reason for the hope that the latter will prevail. Christ identified himself with Truth, and promised to lead his followers into all truth. The sacraments are signposts on the pilgrimage to Him, and the minister, as George Herbert observed, is the deputy of Christ, and himself a pledge of assurance.

Ministry as obedience

One word sums up the different aspects of Ministry that I have been exploring — obedience. It is not a popular or familiar concept in the 1980s. Indeed the thrust of much political activity is to support disobedience and anarchy. Discipline at home and school is challenged and often abandoned with the arrogant claim of every individual to decide for himself what is right and what is wrong. These and many other reasons conspire to remove from obedience those wholesome connotations which ease its acceptance. Of course it does not mean the blind unquestioning acceptance of authority. Yet obedience is a fruit of love. There is not time in the span of one life to question, challenge and determine everything. Much must be taken on trust.

That is particularly true for christians and servants of the church where tradition has built up a common way of life which, not without modification, has proved its worth down the centuries. We speak of the formation of character. The word 'formation' expresses a truth and a process which is equally valid for all discipleship. Many factors play their part in this, not least a regular feeding of the mind and soul on the things of God in prayer — in common prayer which is shared by the rest of the people of God. All of us have our black days, our moods of depression. It is just then that the support of a rule is a literal Godsend. It can provide a well-trodden path which others have found to be a short cut to better times. It can also enrich the efforts of the individual with the sense of corporate activity. In the words of George Herbert:

> Prayer, the Church's banquet, Angels' age,
> God's breath in man returning to his birth,
> The soul in paraphrase, heart in pilgrimage,
> The Christian plummet, sounding heaven and earth

or as Thomas Campion put it:

> Seek the Lord, and in his way persever,
> O faint not, but as eagles fly;
> For his steep hill is high;
> Then striving gain the top, and triumph ever.

The spirit of obedience must inform the whole of our pilgrimage. We have only taken the daily prayer as an example. Obedience is an attitude, it is not blind acceptance. Because it is out of tune with the times it might be thought to have served its purpose and be ready for relegation to the lumber room of ecclesiastical fashions. That can never be so for those who follow the author of the words 'If you love me, you will keep my commandments.'

The state of the Church of England at the beginning of the last century was probably at an all-time low. Yet it was transformed, indeed transfigured, because men and women cared and were ready to spend the time upon the things they cared for. They did not give up when they met opposition. We forget the riots and imprisonments which were concomitants of reform. We are faced with a hard call, a costly one which can seldom be popular and never easy. But for those who love the Church of England and believe in its continuing mission, the need for renewal, personal and institutional, is synonymous with the hope of resurrection.

Peter Moore is Dean of St Albans.

6
Ruling Passion

Trueman Dicken

No more than four or five years ago voices were still to be heard denying that there had been any notable decline in moral standards in Britain during the twentieth century. Today, in the face of soaring statistics of crimes of violence, burglary, vandalism, extra-marital cohabitation, illegitimacy, broken marriages and the rest, doubt is no longer possible, and the public hopes against hope that the moral landslide is attributable to social and economic conditions which can be rectified by appropriate governmental action.

The grounds for such hope are slender. The welfare state affords educational opportunities and insurance against ill-health or destitution on a scale inconceivable at the beginning of the century, while subsidised legal aid protects civil rights which then did not even exist. The average income in this country in real terms increased tenfold between 1900 and 1970[1], and the gap betwen the highest and lowest incomes has narrowed almost unbelievably. Yet throughout the period the rising statistics of crime and misbehaviour have pursued their inexorable way.

Certainly there is evidence to indicate that permissive legislation has accelerated the pace of moral decline, for example in the areas of pornography and obscenity, of deviant sexual practices and of the breakdown of marriage, where the public has drawn the inference that, 'If it isn't illegal, it can't be very wrong'. Yet this is legislation which has come about at the instance of public opinion. It is the reflection rather than a primary cause of our moral malaise.

In this fallen world it should be axiomatic that sin requires no other causes than ignorance, self-interest and infirmity of moral purpose; yet it must be admitted that there are many and diverse pressures in the world of today which compound man's ignorance, appeal to his self-

1. Brian Griffiths: *Morality and the Market Place,* London (Hodder & Stoughton) 1982.

interest and erode his moral will. I would point first to a remarkable alliance, as unholy as it is unintentional, between big money and Marxist activism. Big money aims to sell its products to as many people as possible whether they need them or not, and as a leading figure in the world of advertising has pointed out, 'All advertising's promises can be classified under one or more of the following nine basic drives: self-preservation, love for others, self-expression, envy, sloth, lechery, gluttony, pride, covetousness.' He adds with uninhibited frankness, 'I don't apologise for using six of the seven deadly sins. I've omitted anger — it's used very rarely'[2]. Considering the vast sums of money and the highly competitive expertise brought to bear in commercial marketing to make sin attractive with but small countervailing effort in favour of Christian virtue, one cannot be surprised if it has an effect.

Big money may find little profit in inculcating anger, but the deficiency is more than compensated by the very specific use made of anger, along with the other 'basic drives', in left-wing inspired propaganda. But communist theory actually welcomes the effects of capitalist advertising too; precisely because they are damaging to the present structures of society they cannot but hasten the coming of the proletarian revolution.

There is a second and no less morally deleterious unholy alliance between incompatibles, both of which have so deeply infiltrated our culture that their jargon and slogans are the conversational platitudes of those who know nothing whatever of their origins. It is the unperceived but insidious alliance between Freudianism and existentialist theory.

Freudianism takes its stand on a rigid determinism, which holds that human beings are wholly at the mercy of early influences in their lives and therefore cannot be held responsible for their actions, whilst frustration of the fundamental driving force, the sexual urge, must necessarily impair mental and often physical health. Existentialism on the contrary is almost hysterically anxious to proclaim that man not only can but *must* liberate himself from all external influences, and is responsible to no-one but himself. To conform to conventional rules of conduct is to be less than fully human: one's only duty is to 'do one's own thing'. Whilst the two approaches are logically mutually exclusive, the libidinous and ego-centric (of which there is something in all of us) find no difficulty in making the transition from the Freudian plea, 'I can't help doing this: other people have made me what I am', to the existentialist declaration, 'This is the real me, so this is what I ought to do.'

---

2. David Bernstein: *Creative Advertising,* London (Longmans) 1974.

Set aside many years ago by those most competent to judge, as being alike methodologically deficient and unverifiable, both Freudianism and existentialism have nevertheless continued in close harness for the last forty years to dominate the world of fiction, film and theatre, and through these channels and through 'advice' columns in newspapers and magazines have together largely shaped the new 'morality', above all in the areas of sexual and social behaviour. Their alchemy has made a vice of many virtues, self-restraint and chastity among them, and has been an inexhaustible quarry for controversial material which the media, not surprisingly, find the most saleable of all commodities. It both flatters the customer's confidence in his intellectual perspicacity and enables him to justify his moral shortcomings.

Most regrettably, the Church of England has in recent years been all too ready to follow the secular trend, frequently sponsoring publications which promote controversy by calling in question the Church's firmly-rooted doctrinal and moral teaching rather than seeking to explain and defend it.[3] Almost without noticing it, Anglicanism would seem so far to have aligned itself with many fundamentally humanist tenets as to invest them with almost canonical authority.

An outstanding example of such an innovation is the humanist doctrine of natural rights, surprisingly adopted also by the Second Vatican Council.[4] Few of our contemporaries are any longer aware that the doctrine that all men have an inalienable right to life, liberty and the pursuit of happiness finds no place either in scripture or in the Christian tradition. We owe the wording to Thomas Jefferson in 1776, and the concept itself can be traced back no further than John Locke in the late seventeenth century.[5] For the first nineteen centuries of our era, Christian moral teaching consistently recognised *duties* as the ultimate basis of morality, such rights and privileges as we may have being seen, surely rightly, as essentially no more than derivatives of prior obligations. Can anyone seriously hold, for example, that we have a fundamental right to pursue happiness — irrespective, that is, of the effect this may have on others? Would anyone wish to contend that liberty is the inalienable right of a dangerous killer or rapist? Is it credible that we have a built-in right to life, when the only categorical certainty about any one of us is that we shall die?

---

3. E.g. *The Ordination of Women to the Priesthood* (1972), *Marriage and the Church's Task* (1978), *Homosexual Relationships* (1979) (all Church Information Office Publications).
4. *De Ecclesia in Mundo Hujus Temporis,* I.26 et al.
5. Maurice Cranston: *What are Human Rights?* London (Bodley Head) 1973.

On the other hand, can anyone really doubt that we all have an absolute *duty* not to murder any of our fellow human beings, to violate her or to rob him or her of the necessities of life? Is it also any less clear that, having a duty to heal, a doctor must be allowed the right to handle beneficial though potentially lethal drugs? Given responsibility for the safety of his ship, must not a captain have the right to command obedience from all aboard her? Some rights are unquestionably necessary, but they flow from duties, and it is the duties which are inalienable.

One effect of uncritical acceptance of the fashionable doctrine of human rights has been the embarrassed attitude of the church to the debate on abortion. It is a matter of record that the Abortion Act of 1967 was instigated chiefly by the Women's Rights movement.[6] Effective technical use was made at the time of the 'thalidomide scare', but the basic arguments for what eventuated virtually as abortion on demand were that a woman has a fundamental natural right to determine what happens within her own body, and that it is wrong to allow an unwanted or disadvantaged child to be born, even in its own interests. Almost nothing was said about the unborn infant's right to life. Perhaps rights belong only to those who can personally press for them? In the event, it has been calculated that at least fifteen million healthy unborn babies have been legally aborted all over the world in the past ten years, a rate of destruction of human life roughly equivalent to a new Hiroshima or Nagasaki once a fortnight throughout the same period.

The true nature of abortion is quite clear: a fertilised ovum is by definition a human being from the moment of conception. It is indisputably a discrete being, and equally certainly a human one. If the unborn baby will admittedly be entirely dependent upon his or her mother for the next nine months, he or she will be no less dependent upon the mother, or other human surrogates, for a good many more years. Indeed, no human being can ever cease to depend on others without literally intolerable privation. If it is morally permissible to abort an unborn child simply because it is dependent and an encumbrance, there can be no logical reason not to end the life of any other human being on the same grounds.

It is therefore no accident that the passage of the Abortion Act has been followed by pressure for the legalisation of euthanasia. Once again, appeal is made to a 'natural right of man', on the dubiously logical

---

6. Hindell & Sims: *Abortion Law Reformed*, London, 1968.

grounds that if a human being has a natural right to life, he has also a natural right to death. 'I did not ask to come into this world,' it is pleaded, 'and if I find life hateful or unbearable, there is no good reason why I should not put an end to it'.

Many non-Christians would contest this claim, if only because, by the time a person has reached an age to take any serious decision, parents, relatives, friends and society as a whole have invested too heavily in him for the decision to terminate his life to be one for his own personal discretion: 'You may feel you don't want to live, but *we* want you, and you owe it to us not to do away with yourself.'

Since the Suicide Act of 1961, suicide has ceased to be a crime in this country, but it still remains a criminal offence to help someone to commit suicide, for the obvious and very cogent reason that this could be no more than a subtle way of committing murder. By the same token, a most powerful humanitarian argument against the legalisation of euthanasia is that it would allow unspeakable pressure to be exerted on a desperately sick patient by relatives or friends who wished to ease their own harrowing burdens, or merely to accelerate receipt of a desirable legacy.

Without in the least derogating from these arguments, the Christian should surely add a consideration which, to him, ought to outweigh them all, namely our duty not to reject the life entrusted to us by a loving Creator. We cannot say why we should have to suffer in this way or that, but to refuse to do so is fatally to abandon the faith and hope in God which is the indispensable ground of our salvation. Suicide (and voluntary euthanasia is clearly a form of suicide) may not be a crime, but it is undoubtedly a sin, of which the gravest feature is that it precludes irrevocably all opportunity for repentance.

That this is so adds the greater urgency to our own obligation to alleviate with all the love and skill at our command the suffering of all our fellow men, and it is immensely reassuring to have been shown by Dame Cicely Saunders how, by a combination of dedicated spiritual care and modern medical techniques, the pain and distress of terminal illness can not merely be rendered tolerable but given positive value for the dying patient.[7] Ought not this to be given the highest priority in the deloyment of our humanly limited medical resources?

The fact is that in any event, for the Christian, the issues of abortion and euthanasia call for no agonising or tortuous debate if it is simply borne in mind that we all have an unconditional duty not to kill a

---

7. Cicely Saunders & Mary Baines: *Living with Dying,* Oxford (OUP) 1983.

defenceless and innocent human being, even on the pretext that it is in his own interests to do so. One need be no cynic to recognise that the next item on the agenda after abortion and voluntary euthanasia would be involuntary euthanasia.

Present day trends in this direction nevertheless already pose a peculiarly acute dilemma for the medical practitioner. How could he retain the confidence of his patients in his integrity as a healer if doctors become recognised as privileged death-dealers? On reflection, the thought must be even more disturbing for the patients than for the doctor.

This particular dilemma in the field of medical ethics has indeed a further significance. It exemplifies neatly the dangers of a phenomenon which permeates our modern culture at every level, namely the confusion of roles within society. The subject merits our closer attention in view of its far-reaching ramifications.

Much is made at the present day of the 'crisis of identity', diagnosed as a major cause of social alienation among our contemporaries. The cliché fails accurately to define the problem. Whoever I am, I know that I am me. What I may not be at all sure of is my actual or potential relationship with other people: I may be confused, that is to say, about either my own role or about theirs as it affects me, and most probably about both. The confusion is heightened by the abandonment, if not intentional suppression, of an infinite variety of signals which in years gone by were indicators of roles. Sweaters and jeans are as likely to be worn off-duty by the barrister as by the barrow-boy, the university professor's accent may be identical with that of his scouse-speaking former school friend, and a bishop may encourage the scruffiest choirboy to call him Joe.

Whatever the social or economic causes of this levelling, it finds both its rationale and a massive emotional impetus to its further extension in the humanist egalitarianism of our day. Aiming to liberate twentieth century men and women from anything resembling type-casting or a social caste system, it nevertheless produces its own, often severe, frustrations. People are not like so many grains of rice in a pudding. They are not interchangeable at random, and it is difficult to see how either things or persons can properly be said to be equal unless they *are* interchangeable. If the individual is to have *any* place in society, it must be a particular place of his own. Without one, both his emotional security and his ability to make any effective contribution to the purposes of society are gravely at risk.

Christian recognition of this fact has traditionally been subsumed in the assertion that God does love every one of us infinitely and individually. It is a glorious truth, but in no way does it argue that we either are or ought to be equal. On the contrary, it is extraordinary that in recent times the Church should have undermined its own crucial understanding of the doctrine of the body of Christ, whose members are widely diverse and disparate yet all indispensable within the Church,[8] by *de facto* acceptance of egalitarian rhetoric which finds minimal support in holy writ.[9] As both psychologists and anthropologists have made us well aware, any society is and must be functionally structured, and depends for its very survival on the stability of an intricate pattern of reciprocating relationships between members whose roles must be both easily recognisable and accepted within the community as a whole.[10]

A highly pertinent example of the effect of confusion of roles is to be seen in the consequences of the claim, openly asserted as it now is, that relationships of all kinds with those of one's own sex ought to be socially and morally on a parity with heterosexual ones. Just how unrealistic this is becomes evident from the mere consideration that the success of even so 'unFreudian' a situation as a formal dinner party requires the alternate seating of men and women round the table. Nevertheless, although any individual's exclusive preference for persons either of his own sex or the other is indicative of a degree of social maladjustment, it is not necessarily in itself a threat to moral order.

Regrettably, 'gay' propaganda has enjoyed a good deal of success in lumping together in the public mind mere partiality for the company of one's own sex under one head with habitual homosexual genital activity as a way of life and with all else in between, accounting them all clear contra-indications to marriage. Given that almost every human being sooner or later goes through one or more homosexual phases, expecially in adolescence, one bitterly cruel result of this tendentious disinformation has been to convince an unascertainable but certainly immense number of normal youngsters, experiencing even a mildly homosexual phase, that they are actually constitutionally and irreversibly homosexual. Weltering in guilty feelings, they can become trapped for life in the desperately isolating existence of those so grievously misnamed 'gay'.

---

8. Romans 12:3-9; I Corinthians 12:4-31 et al.
9. The concept of equality as understood today is quite alien to both the Old Testament and the New. Even II Corinthians 8:14 argues only that impoverished Christians ought not to be allowed by their richer brethren to go in want.
10. Cf e.g. Michael Argyle: *The Psychology of Interpersonal Behaviour,* London (Pelican) 1967; H. Garfinkel: *Studies in Ethnomethodology,* New York (Prentice Hall) 1967.

Leaders of Christian thought must frankly bear a heavy share of responsibility for this state of affairs,[11] which has ruined innumerable marriages and denied to countless individuals the happiness which marriage can bring. Anxious to appear both compassionate and very up-to-date, the church has failed to make clear that, on the most unmistakable of biblical and theological grounds, whilst homosexual genital acts are sinful,[12] unsought homosexual proclivities are not. Sin is a matter of what we *do,* not of what we are tempted to do.

One suspects that the failure to grasp and make clear these points stems from a still more serious error, by which the crucial and truly liberating message of the Gospel that no sinner is beyond forgiveness and redemption has been misconstrued as minimising the whole gravity of sin. Christ's teaching is categorical: all sins can be forgiven, none can be condoned. Any sin can by the grace of God be overcome, but only if it is recognised for what it is and abjured. To dilute or misrepresent this vital understanding cannot but bring about untold damage in many areas of human activity quite apart from sexual ones.

It is unfashionable to say so, but the overcoming of any sin calls for self-denial and self-restraint — painful virtues which can only painfully be learnt, but which by the divine grace progressively bring that freedom from sin which is the glorious liberty of the children of God. It is the Church's calling to be the catalyst in this process. The great classical teachers of Christian spirituality understood well what had to be done, and it is to them, not to the modern exponents of a secularised or syncretistic 'new spirituality' that the Church must return to recover her direction and pastoral effectiveness.

It cannot be said too often that neither Christian moral discernment nor Christian moral conduct are to be had without the faith and spirituality with which they are inseparably bound up. Morality cannot be reduced to a computerised system for disgorging school solutions to impersonally stated moral dilemmas: it can be learnt only by living and, as the much undervalued prayer-book catechism rightly says, by praying. It depends upon patterns of thought and behaviour developed by following the ground-rules year in and year out until they become second nature.

Despite all impressions to the contrary, moreover, Christianity is not dedicated to ideals. Ideals are seldom attainable. Traditional

---

11. Especially influential was Norman Pittenger: *Time for Consent,* London (SCM) 1970.
12. Leviticus 18:22; 20:13; Romans 1:27; I Timothy 1:9-10 et al.

Christianity sets before us values and standards which are within reach of all, although their concomitant requirements become apparent only as we learn to live by them: don't harm your fellow human beings, don't steal from them or cheat them, don't lie to them, don't abuse their sexual integrity, don't above all be led further astray by envying them. These are standards which are doubtless best learnt starting from childhood in the context of a stable family life, but since they are the standards which still lie at the very heart of Western culture, they are by no means beyond recovery among the adult population of our country today. Because they reflect the purpose of *one* God, the unique source of all that is and also its redeemer and sanctifier, they have a cohesion and self-consistency in which modern secular and humanist ethics are strikingly deficient.

This last observation deserves to be underlined. In moral matters twentieth century man unthinkingly embraces mutually exclusive theories, pursues incompatible objectives and ends in moral confusion and failure. In the realm of science he enjoys notably better success precisely because the scientist always seeks the most economical hypothesis to explain his findings, on the assumption that there is an underlying unity in all things. The assumption appears to be well justified, and is increasingly acknowledged to be a derivative of the monotheistic religious culture in which alone scientific learning grew up. Is it not reasonable to suppose that the same assumption is essential to sound moral order?

The Church cannot impose this moral order or enforce its standards, even if it were right that it should try to do so. It can teach them, and its teachings will impress if its members live by them; but the evidence suggests strongly that it will achieve nothing unless it gives its own firmly rooted vision of God's absolute priority over the 'exciting new insights' of contemporary humanism. To topple the priorities in the interests of dialogue with the multiple society is both to compromise our own integrity and to destroy the whole validity of what we have to say.

Trueman Dicken was formerly a lecturer in theology at the University of Nottingham.

7
Unholy matrimony

Margaret Hewitt

Do we really believe what we say? Do we even listen to what it said? In Church, men and women vow 'to have and to hold from this day forward, for better for worse, for richer for poorer, in sickness and in health, to love and to cherish, till death us do part, according to God's holy ordinance'. In Registry Offices, it is the practice of registrars to remind couples 'of the solemn and binding character of the vows you are about to undertake.' Marriage according to the laws of this country is the union of one man and one woman, voluntarily entered into for life to the exclusion of others. Yet in the past ten years our divorce rate has multiplied five times so that one in three marriages end that way.

Increase in divorce is common in all modern European experience, but so high a divorce rate as ours is unique in the West. Recently, a Russian commentator revealed an equally high rate had been reached in the Soviet Union and declared that it signalled the death of marriage as an institution. Our own experience prompts an alternative observation: the institution of marriage is not dying, but official definitions of it are now more idealistic than realistic. Marriage remains an extremely — historically, extraordinarily — popular institution. Writing of *Marriage in Britain - 1945-1980* Dr Dominian traced the fluctuation of marriage rates in the period 1970-1977 and concludes 'the popularity of marriage, despite these fluctuations, can be seen by looking at the figures of the ever married. This shows that by the age of 49 the ever married in England and Wales were consistently 90% for men and . . . there has been a steady rise in the last fifty years of women ever married, increasing from 83% in 1931 to 93% in 1974.'[1]

The widespread publicity given to the increasing vulnerability of marriage seems not to have daunted those eligible to enter the married state. 'Once bitten, twice shy' scarcely describes the attitude to marriage of those who have actually experienced divorce. The number of

---

1. *Marriage in Britain, 1945-80*, Dr J. Dominian, Study Commission of the Family.

marriages between a man and woman, one of whom has been divorced, has risen from 1 in 5 to 1 in 3 in the last decade. In 1978, 1 in 10 marriages were marriages where both had been divorced. Today, about half those who divorce re-marry within five years of doing so. Alas! Second time around is even more hazardous. Forty per cent of all second marriages end in divorce. And yet some try — and try — again, thus giving substance to the belief that 'serial marriage' is replacing 'life-long' marriage in this country.

Historians are quick to point out that 'serial marriage' is no new phenomenon in England. One in three of all marriages in Stuart England, for example, were second or later marriages. (According to the 1688 records of one parish, 39% of marriages solemnised were with a partner married before; 13% were second marriages; 3% were third marriages; 4% were fourth — and one person had five previous partners!) But this is 'serial marriage' of a very different kind. The critical difference being that death played then the part that divorce does now. As one sociologist puts it: 'the divorce court inherits the function of the undertaker'. But why?

There are, and always have been, 'difficult' marriages. There is no evidence for a 'Golden Age' of matrimony. It is therefore not unreasonable to ask whether there has in fact been a real increase in marriage breakdown or whether marriages that broke down in the past are now, or most of them, seeking a formal divorce instead of relying on death or desertion. Has the increase in divorce been simply a movement from informal and formal separation to divorce mainly as a result of more 'liberal' divorce laws and easier legal aid?

We have no means of knowing the incidence of marital breakdown in the past but the evidence supports more than a hypothesis that the divorce figures simply reflect the increase of marriage in a larger population and easier financial support for divorce. 'The most plausible explanation of the divorce figures for the past two decades', writes Chester, 'is that they are related to social and cultural changes much more fundamental than amendments to the terms of somewhat limited welfare schemes.'[2] But what are these changes?

Many will argue that the greatly increased expectation of life during this present century has inevitably made marriage more hazardous since it is longer 'at risk'. Boys born in 1901 could expect to live until they were 48 years of age; girls born in the same year could expect to live until they

---

2. *Divorce and Legal Aid – A False Hypothesis*, R. Chester, *Sociology* 6.205, 1972.

were 52. In 1978 this life-expectation was increased to 70 for boys and 78 for girls. Another way of pointing to the same development as it affects marriage is to express the expectation of life of those aged twenty, which for the United Kingdom during the years 1974-76 was 51.3 years for men and 57.1 for women. This length of marriage, longer than the total life-span of the men and women of earlier generations, certainly those born in Stuart times, makes it 'obvious' that permanency of marriage is no longer attainable in contemporary society. No two people could be expected to sustain or endure one relationship if it lasts so long. But if mere length of marriage is the critical factor in the explanation of the current rate of divorce, why is it that the highest rate of divorce is among those more recently married? Why is there no mid-life 'peak', with more divorces after fifteen or twenty years of marriage?

Age at marriage, rather than length of marriage, clearly is sometimes adduced as the reason for the overwhelming incidence of marital breakdown in the early rather than the later years of marriage. Certainly it is true that the younger people marry the more likely they are to get divorced. But the records show that from the early 1970s there have been falls in the marriage rates of the youngest age groups; and an evident trend since 1976 towards people marrying later. The divorce rate, however, has shown no tendency to decrease; rather the reverse.

Since childless marriages are generally thought to be more vulnerable than others it is worth noting that many women now choose to have their children later than they used to, and asking whether the noticeable brevity of many marriages is related to this fact. Put another way: do children 'hold a marriage together'? There is considerable difficulty in answering 'yes' to such a question. In the first place, it is true that the median interval between marriage and the birth of the first child increased from 20 months in 1971 to 30 months in 1979. The majority of marriages break down within four years or after a child has been born. In the second place, if one analyses the divorces which took place in 1979, 6 out of every 10 couples divorced had children under 16, of whom half were between the ages of 5 and 10 and almost a quarter under the age of 5.

Does the vastly increased number of married women out at work, which now includes a very considerable number of mothers of young children, affect the issue — a question which also raises the allegation that the 'independence' of modern women undermines the institution of marriage. Clashes of interest between the claims of the workplace and those of home and family are all too evident to those who study the experience of women at work but the evidence is lacking which could substantiate the claim that these are the root causes of most divorces — just as it is lacking as a root cause of child neglect. Some would even claim that an 'outside interest' actually helps to sustain a marriage and that it is the 'captive wife' who is most at risk. We simply do not know. What we do know for certain is that, no doubt to the chagrin of Women's Liberation, for far and away the majority of women, marriage is as much their main objective in life as it was for their Victorian forebears. Women's paid employment is seen by them as supplementing, not providing, the family income. The promotion and personal advancement of wives at work is subordinated to the promotion and personal advancement of their husbands, as anyone who employs — or seeks to employ — married women very well knows.

The fact of the matter is that no one of the factors reviewed above can be claimed as *the* reason why so many more people divorce now than they did ten, twenty, fifty, a hundred years ago. Even taken together they do not fundamentally answer the question 'why?' men and women now choose to turn to the divorce court rather than await the undertaker to terminate their marriage. They are symptoms not merely of the increased complexity of marriage as an institution but of a profoundly different expectation of it than anything entertained by earlier generations. More is expected from marriage than ever before. Men and women expect, and are expected, to find self-fulfilment not the fulfilment of family ambition in marriage. Above all, they seek that elusive prize 'Happiness'. 'Wishing you every Happiness' is the message of the thousands of greetings cards despatched to 'happy couples' in anticipation of the 'happy day'. Happiness for themselves. 'One explanation of what is happening today, is that far too much stress is being laid on the person side of companionship . . . Demanding more . . . people may get more . . . and if people don't get the quality of companionship they expect they move on.'[3] They know they can and they do. It is not too much to say that there is a developed belief that they should; a belief which the Church apparently shares and to the development of which it has contributed substantially in its public utterances in recent years.

Take for example *Putting Asunder*, the all-too-correctly entitled report of a group commissioned by Dr Ramsey, then Archbishop of Canterbury, and chaired by the late Dr Mortimer, then Bishop of

---

3. *Marriage, Love, Sex and Divorce*, Jonathan Gathorne-Hardy, Jonathan Cape, 1981.

Exeter. The task was:

> ... to review the law of England concerning divorce and, 'recognising that there is a difference in the attitudes of the Church and the State towards the further marriage of a divorced person whose former partner is living, to consider whether the inclusion of any new principle or procedure in the law of the State would be likely to operate:
> (1) more justly and with greater assistance to the durability of marriage and the happiness of all concerned including the children than at present: and
> (2) in such a way as to do nothing to undermine the approach of couples to marriage as a life-long covenant.'

Published in 1966, it was this Report which gave prominence to the concept of 'irretrievable breakdown of marriage' not just as an acceptable, but the one acceptable, ground for divorce in secular law of this country. It recommended the concept of the 'matrimonial offence' of 'guilty' and 'innocent' parties should be abandoned and replaced by 'no fault' divorce legislation.

In the light of evidence submitted to them, particularly evidence from those most nearly connected to administering the current divorce law, the Commission had become convinced that the distinction between 'guilt' and 'innocence' was 'wholly preposterous'. It appeared that 'the law is moving away from basing divorce on a finding concerning the delinquency of one of the parties towards basing it on a finding concerning the state of the marriage relationship and the demands of distributive justice. In other words, it is feeling its way to the doctrine of the breakdown of marriage.[4]. . . In our judgement the change in the law we recommend would have very little effect on the general conception of marriage, since the belief that marriage is "perishable" is already widely entertained and is encouraged by developments in the administration of the existing law.'[5]

'Irretrievable breakdown of marriage' was the concept which was to dominate the subsequent discussion of possible ways of reforming our divorce laws; by the Divorce Law Reform Act, 1969, which came into force in 1971, it became the sole ground on which a petition for divorce may be presented.

True, the authors of *Putting Asunder* expressly stated that their appointed task was to consider the law necessary in secular society:

---

4. *Putting Asunder: Report of a Group Appointed by the Archbishop of Canterbury, 1966*, p. 37.
5. ibid. p. 43.

> How the doctrine and discipline of Christ concerning marriage should be interpreted and applied within the Church is one question; what the Church ought to say and do about secular laws of marriage and divorce is another question altogether. This can hardly be repeated too often . . . Anyone speaking on behalf of the Church who fails to observe the distinction there made is bound to be misunderstood both within the Church and in society at large.

Almost inevitably, the Church was 'misunderstood'. People — both within the Church and in society at large — read the Press headlines, not the small print of the documents they refer to. 'It is difficult to explain to anyone, above all those who have never studied the Report, that the Established Church was advising the State to enact legislation flatly contrary to her own doctrine . . .', wrote Dr Trueman Dicken. 'Simple and far from simple minds cannot fairly be blamed for supposing, however erroneously, that what the Church recommended, the Church approved of.'[6] The Church was understandably taken to be more interested in answering the question 'How can we as Christians help people with difficult marriages to separate more happily and easily?' instead of the far more important question for both Church and State, 'How far can we help people to be faithful in marriage, given there is divorce in this country?'

It has to be said that Dr Mortimer's group were emphatic that there should be a very thorough court investigation of alleged matrimonial breakdown. But the recommendation was rejected by the Law Commission as procedurally impracticable. It also has to be said that the group expressed a concern that the interests of the children of the marriage should be protected. In the event, their interests have been considered almost exclusively in economic terms; in the light of evidence that the marriage of which they were the fruits has become intolerable to their parents. What they themselves think may be a different matter. Research has shown that large numbers of them consider their homes were happy or very happy before divorce.[7]

It is extraordinary that the Commission should have been so ingenuous as to write: 'we have no reason to believe that the entire substitution of breakdown for the matrimonial offence would, in the long run, make divorce easier or increase the number of decrees granted to any significant extent.'[8] Intent on removing any remaining 'prejudice' against divorcees they should surely have realised that the result could

---

6. *The Undermining of Marriage*, Dr E. W. Trueman Dicken, *For Better For Worse*, 1971.
7. cf. Gathorne-Hardy, op. cit.
8. *Putting Asunder*, p. 59.

only be to make divorce itself even more acceptable. Subsequent experience has proved this all too true. Divorce in this country is now very easy indeed. Undefended petitions — common enough in the 1960s — are now so common as to be increasingly dealt with by post: a 'painless' and cheap procedure. To 'speed things up' and to meet the growing number of petitions for the consideration of a divorce petition after only one year of marriage, instead of the three normally required under present legislation, the Law Commission are now proposing that what is now 'exceptional' should in future become generally available.

The implications of such a proposal have been seen very clearly by the Board for Social Reponsibility, whose Chairman, the Bishop of Birmingham, has already labelled the present rate of divorce in this country 'a national disaster'. In a very pithily worded report, *Time Restrictions on Presentations of Divorce and Nullity Petitions* (1983) the point is made:

> The most urgent need is not to extend the present practice for divorce earlier than the three year rule, but for serious consideration to be given to adequate support for marriage growth and development, and for appropriate professional research to be made available to support this . . . It is the duty of the community, if we wish marriage to succeed, to do all in our power to provide for such success. We might add that it is also the duty of the community to frame its law so that couples are encouraged to make their marriage in this sense.

Exactly: and it is no less the duty of the Church to bend every effort to the same end. What has the Church been busying itself doing during the past decade? Bending its mind to modifying its marriage discipline so as to incorporate the 'new understanding' of marriage in late twentieth century society. Commending 'the irretrievable breakdown of marriage', so successfully commended as a principle of secular divorce legislation, as a theologically acceptable reason for allowing a divorced partner to be married in Church to a fresh partner whilst their previous partner still lives. Whatever else may be said of this, Church discipline flows from Church doctrine and whatever linguistic stratagems are adopted to fudge the issue, what has been commended in the Root Report *Marriage, Divorce and the Church*, and more recently by the Bishop of Lichfield's Commission in *Marriage and the Church's Task* is in open conflict with existing Canon Law.

Marriage, Divorce and the Church was the report of a Commission specifically instructed 'to prepare a statement on the Christian doctrine of marriage'. Unlike the group which prepared *Putting Asunder*, and made its recommendations for secular society on the understanding, however unfortunate, that a non-Christian society could not be expected to accept Christian standards, *Marriage, Divorce and the Church* appears to base its recommendations on the major premise that the Church cannot be effective in its mission to society unless it abides by the standards and practices of that society. For example, *Putting Asunder* raised the possible need for some modification of the existing relationship between Church and State as a consequence of reform of the secular law of divorce. *Marriage, Divorce and the Church* rejects the possibility of the adoption here of a long-standing practice in some other European countries of marriage by universal registration followed by solemnisation in church. It comments:

> In the event of the State legislating for two kinds of marriage, civil and ecclesiastical, the one dissoluble, the other not, a lesser and more restricted intention would be imputed by those marrying by civil process than those whose weddings would be solemnised in church.[9]

As matters stand, however, the one marriage is dissoluble and the other not and herein lies the nub of the problem. Since there has not — as yet — been a proposal to rescind Canon B 30, how is the Church to accommodate the will of God to the laws of Man? Apparently by linking the former with the outlook of the latter.

In the section on the *Institution of Marriage,* the Report asserts:

> The Church enshrines, therefore, in its liturgy certain truths about marriage — that it is lifelong, that it is exclusive . . . The church has to be sometimes, as it has had to be in history, a voice of witness for these truths even against the nation, against forces, whether in the mind or in the exercise of political or other power, which make it excessively difficult for people to perceive them or to live by them. There is an inevitable tension between the Church and society as well as natural accord.[10]

How very curious then that in a final section on *Strengthening Marriage* we find the recommendation that those whose first marriages have been terminated by divorce should be allowed to re-marry in church with what is substantially the same service, making the same vows 'till death us do part'. The explanation lies in their approach to the problems of marriage in terms of personal relationships rather than theoretical assumptions. They have chosen to switch from orthodox theology to praxis theology: to set aside agreed doctrine in favour of situational ethics.

Hence ideas canvassed for approval in *Marriage, Divorce and the Church* in 1971 were commended as guides for action in *Marriage and the Church's*

---

9. ibid. p. 69.
10. ibid. p. 59.

Task seven years later. Astonishingly — although in the light of their recommendations, understandably — the authors 'refused to see (in Jesus's own teaching) either legislation or direct pastoral instruction (on marriage) although some of us believe they must have some legislative import and hence a bearing on matters of pastoral discipline.'[11] Marriage, they assert, 'is best understood as "for" husband and wife (not "for" children). It is *their* relationship which is the basis of marriage.'[12] The group asked themselves: 'What practical response is likely to meet the needs of individual men and women, while at the same time doing justice to our fundamental perception of what marriage should be?' Their answer echoes that of the Root Commission: if the relationship turns out for worse rather than better, try again in the context of the same liturgy. It was the answer accepted by General Synod at York in 1981.

This is not the place to examine yet again either the theological arguments surrounding the concept of indissolubility or the various proposals debated at York in July 1983 for putting into effect the view that 'in certain (undefined) circumstances' the Church would allow the marriage in church of divorced people whilst a previous partner was still living. It is however the time for the Church to ask itself whether its task of 'promoting in our society an understanding of Christian marriage' (*Marriage and the Church's Task*) would be better assisted by helping married people to stay married rather than to re-marry. Douglas Brown recently proposed in the *Church Times* that the Church should 'concentrate briefly on marriage itself as the most enduring of human institutions. And we should ask ourselves if the Church could not do more to prevent something like one in three marriages in this country ending in divorce . . . There is no escaping the criticism of social historians [he might have added of sociologists] that Churches usually manage to accommodate themselves to the prevailing *mores* of society. And among the more prevailing *mores* of our society are easy divorce and, for that matter, easy abortion — attitudes conditioned by a mix of pluralism, casuistry and secularism.'

Social historians reflect on the past; sociologists speculate about the future. Probably few of them would describe themselves as 'indissolubilists' (even supposing they knew what that meant), but many would and do question the wisdom of a marriage-support which can only add to its fragility. There can be no doubt whatsoever that easier secular divorce has contributed substantially to an increased rate of

---

11. *Marriage and the Church's Task, 1978,* p. 44.
12. ibid. p. 33.

divorce both here and in every country which has pursued the same policy. Can it seriously be believed that a second — or third, or fourth marriage in Church will have no similar effect? Does the Church neither itself attach any credence to the vows, unaltered, its own marriage services require, nor expect anyone else to do so? How can the charge of causistry or near blasphemy be rebutted with either intellectual or moral integrity?

Additionally, one might press the question, Does the right hand of the Church pay any attention to what its left hand is doing? Has it actually got a co-ordinated strategy for 'promoting in our society a Christian understanding of marriage?' General Synod voted in the July of 1981 for the principle of re-marriage in Church. Not until October 1982 did the House of Bishops resolve to establish a panel of advisors on marriage preparation and support and to appoint a full-time Advisor in Marriage Education. The observation 'too little, too late' springs all too readily to mind — or is it 'shutting the stable door after the horse has gone'? One could wish for a more robust approach to cope with a 'national disaster'. Contrast the actions of the interdenominational Order for Christian Unity and its evidence to the Lord Chancellor's committee on conciliation and matrimonial law. The Order did not hesitate to suggest that the committee was asking the wrong questions. It was looking at *conciliation:* the process of estrangement, of a married couple separating, whereas the Order believed that the principal need is for *reconciliation:* healing breakdowns and saving marriages. It urged a variant of a proposal made years ago in *Putting Asunder*, but rejected then, that the State take seriously the view that not all divorces are actually necessary.

Putting Asunder had assumed a concern on the part of the State that divorce should be the last, not the first, concern of legislators. In practice there is little or no sign that the Government values marriage as an important social institution and there is almost total lack of interest in sustaining marriage. In consequence, voluntary agencies have emerged to undertake a task either declined or discounted by the State and, as the Chairman of the Order for Christian Unity rightly claims, where machinery for reconciliation has been available it has been a proven success.

Marriage Repair illustrates what can be done. Set up in 1981 in Bristol by a group of private individuals as a voluntary counselling service, it handled 200 enquiries in the first year of work and claims an apparent 'success' rate of around 80% where both husband and wife sought counsel. The Order for Christian Unity, in their submission to the Lord Chancellor's committee, advocated an extension of *Marriage Repair* on a national basis with branches affiliated to the 600 local magistrates courts and that the law should be amended, 'not with the aim of making divorce more difficult but of making sure that it is really necessary in any given case — or, put another way, ensuring that good marriages are not wasted.'[13] Since the Courts Conciliation Service and the Marriage Guidance Council are clearly not between them having sufficient effect on the soaring divorce rate this surely is an enterprise not only worth the wholehearted support of the Church but one with which its official 'establishment' should publicly associate.

So many times one hears that 'the man in the street' pays particular attention to what the Church says and does. What the Church is presently saying and doing about marriage appears a confusion of hypocrisy and self-delusion as public comment and correspondence after the 1983 General Synod decision to set up procedures to enable men and women to marry a second — or third, or fourth — time in church very clearly proves. To the 'man in the street' and to a great number of those in the pew it simply doesn't make sense to witness to 'the total commitment of marriage' by allowing the re-marriage in church of divorced people undertaking the same life-long vows as those marrying for the first time. Of course the Church needs to show a real understanding of those whose marriage has failed: of course the Church must show compassion for their distress, but understanding and indulgence are not the same thing — neither is compassion best comprehended in casuistry.

Margaret Hewitt is reader in sociology at the University of Exeter and chairman of the catholic group in the General Synod of the Church of England.

---

13. *Church Times*, April 15, 1983.

8
Maculate conceptions

Duncan Mitchell

When on July 14, 1833 the Reverend John Keble preached on national apostasy he was recalling the Church of England to its divine vocation, to the realities of the sacraments, and its members to a holy life. On the hundred and fiftieth anniversary last year, Archbishop Huddleston also preached in Oxford but his call was for the Chuch to be involved with others in what he described as a truly Catholic manner. He argued that there should no longer be an authoritarian response to the moral and ethical issues which scientific and technological change gives rise to.

It is not easy to see precisely what he would have us do, but he did say that 'some kind of moral or ethical body in which *all* the expertise now available can be brought together' would be the way forward. Whilst one cannot doubt the usefulness of debate and discussion among informed people, the use of experts and the sifting of evidence, there is no escape from the assertion of moral values. Yet the problem facing us is the multiplicity of values in our national society. Nevertheless, the Church should be of one mind on what is right conduct and to this end it must make authoritative statements from time to time for the benefit of the faithful, if not for others. One subject where changes are taking place as a result of modern science and technology is human reproduction with consequences for marriage and family life; a subject of prime importance to Christian people.

It was in July 1978 that Mr Patrick Steptoe and Dr Robert Edwards announced their success in helping a married couple to have a child by in-vitro fertilisation (IVF) of the wife's oocyte by her husband's sperm and the embryo re-implanted in her uterus to grow so that she gave birth to a healthy daughter. Five years and over a hundred babies later they declared in-vitro fertilisation could be more successful than natural conception, producing fewer abnormal babies. Such is the progress of science and technology. However, this is but the tip of the ice-berg, for more and more developments are taking place in human reproduction and these techniques can be employed for all kinds of purposes both within the marital relationship and outside it.

Of course other forms of artificial reproduction have been practised and for a much longer time. Artificial insemination by husband (AIH) or by donor (AID) are cases in point, and more recently surrogate motherhood. But IVF may take place with donated oocytes fertilised by a husband's semen and the embryo implanted in his wife's uterus. It should be said that Steptoe and Edwards have set their face against this practice, but others have not. Indeed, a donated embryo may be implanted where both semen and oocyte were obtained from others than the husband and wife, so that there is no genetic link between the husband and the wife and the child she bears. It is on these, and cognate matters, that the Church must make up its mind, for the issue concerns marriage and family life. The time has come when the Church needs to be clear as to what is the essential nature of the family. The tendency has been to accommodate itself more and more to a secular view of marriage, a futher step having lately been taken to allow some divorcees to remarry in church, but it is inadequately prepared for further threats to this social institution which some forms of artificial reproduction present. For example, the Archbishop of Canterbury's Commission set up in 1945 to examine AID recommended in 1948 that it be made a crime. A few years later this view was much modified by another Church enquiry, and later the evidence presented to the Warnock Committee by the Board of Social Responsibility was uncertain, pointing out that there are differing and conflicting views on the part of Christians.

Whilst it is usually unwise to try to determine people's rights, the fact remains that not only in the popular mind, but in a declaration by the European Commission on Human Rights, it is held to be a natural right for a married couple to have children. It follows that couples who have difficulties in this respect should be helped. However, long before the European Commission was formed medical practitioners were in fact providing an AID service, and in most cases doing so because of the infertility of the husband, but in a few cases to avoid a genetically transmissible disease such as Huntington's Chorea. Today an AID service is not infrequently provided because a man has had an irreversible vasectomy during a first marriage, then has been divorced and remarried; his second wife requiring a child she has recourse to AID. We see that not only does technology change and develop but social situations change and bring about new demands. The interplay between technology and human desires is such that many more new and different situations are going to arise with concomitant new demands on those who supply the services. What, we may ask, are the moral considerations?

John Keble might well have begun by asking questions about the nature and dignity of man, about the sacramental nature of marriage and the desirability of that quietness of life which is conducive to worship. And perhaps we should ask these questions ourselves, but it would appear that the last quarter of the twentieth century prompts us to ask social questions as well, for clearly they do have a bearing on moral judgements. The main social objection to artificial reproduction, where other than a husband's sperm and his wife's oocyte is concerned, is the secrecy usually attendant on it. Most AID couples do not tell their child about his genetic origin, and in this they stand in contrast to adoptive parents. Moreover, they usually do not tell their own parents with the result that one pair of grandparents rightly believe they are genetically linked to the child whilst the other pair are wrongfully permitted to believe the same about themselves. It is likely that where donated oocytes are used to produce a child the same deception occurs.

This deception of the child, the couple's parents and the community at large cannot be regarded as morally justifiable. In practical terms the child may be misled about his genetic history; a factor of information not without importance for the treatment of diseases. In social terms there are dangers from the strains and stresses of keeping the matter secret, although obviously these may vary in seriousness from couple to couple, but these too must be taken into account. Moreover, the secret may inadvertently be disclosed by a chance remark, or during an angry altercation, or by the intelligent child perceiving some inconsistencies in blood-groupings or eye-colour. The fact is that a couple whose policy is to keep AID a secret finds it progressively harder to tell their kindred later. But the really serious social objection to secrecy is its potential effect on children in normal families, for with greater prominence being given to artificial reproduction, and with its increasing incidence (up to 15% of marriages are infertile), children in normal families may ask seriously (and not as a childish fantasy): 'Is my father really my father?' The child, knowing that AID families practise secrecy, cannot be sure of the veracity of any answer he is given. In short the deception practised in artificial reproduction using donated oocytes or sperm is inimical to one of the family's chief functions, namely the raising of children to be honest and truthful; these are basic qualities of human society which are primarily instilled into children in their families.

The Church has long been a champion of the family; indeed it frequently speaks of itself as the Christian Family of God. Of course, we have to admit that there have been many crimes committed in the name of the family — feuds for example. There has frequently been a glorification of family to the exclusion of other unities and responsibilities. 'My family right or wrong' has seemed a justifiable loyalty to some people. But even allowing for the darker side of familism, it has to be recognised that human society is family-based. However, artificial reproduction may aid lesbian couples and single women to have children. Surrogate motherhood may relieve a woman of the burden of bearing a child but give her the child she wants with husband's sperm and her own oocyte. Artificial reproduction may provide a single woman with a child using her own oöcyte and donated semen. What effect will this have on children, not only those who are the result of this process, but those in normal families where the parents are of opposite sex? Is it desirable? Can it be permitted without detriment to society? There is plenty of evidence that children need a parent of each sex for their own emotional growth and welfare. The proliferation of so-called single-parent families in addition to those resulting from divorce may be said to produce an increase in behavioural problems among children. Hence on social grounds we may advance arguments in favour of normal family life and against some forms of artificial reproduction.

The Church of England's move towards accommodating divorced people who wish to remarry in Church merely adds to the difficulties of maintaining family life at an adequate level of personal commitment and integrity. The reason for saying this is that marriage is rooted in family life. Marriage is fundamentally about children. It is a public declaration by a couple about their responsibilities to the offspring of their union. Hitherto marriage has assured the child that he is who he is; it gives him an identity. When we ask, as we all do sometime, and children in particular, 'Who am I?' the answer we give is made with reference to place and people. 'I was born in such and such a place and my father and mother are so and so.' The basic identity of a child depends upon a truthful knowledge of his origins, for he has a history which is normally known. Such knowledge is received in trust. A child does not undertake historical research although to be sure sometimes curious adults may trace their genealogical history. Most of us believe what we are told or led to believe was the case. How can a child have the dignity of a person and the identity of selfhood if he is created by persons who want a child so much that they are prepared to mislead and deceive him about his birth?

In the case of AID the correct procedure on registering the birth is to state 'father unknown' but invariably the AID couple put down the husband's name. Of course, if the correct procedure were to be followed there would be no secrecy and the couple would then have to go through the process of adopting the child. Doubtless, the secrecy attending AID is designed to protect the husband, possibly the wife, but usually the argument is that it protects the child. If the child were of prime concern perhaps the couple would remain childless or turn to adoption. Proposals to abolish illegitimacy to avoid this problem of registration are ill-conceived. It is not possible to abolish illegitimacy without abolishing legitimacy, which is the safeguard of married couples and the essence of marriage itself, for as we have stated marriage is a public declaration about the offspring of a union being the legal responsibility of the couple. However, the Report of the Warnock Committee published in July 1984 recommended that the AID child be deemed legitimate.

If we are to look further into the moral problem which presents itself we must ask questions about ourselves and our motives. Are we putting our needs above those of others? And are these needs really needs or are they wants and desires which we have acquired? When the sex ratio at the end of the last century was unequal and became more so after 1914, many women were unable to marry, but they accepted not only their spinsterhood but their childlessness. With the decline of religion both within as well as without the Church a new secular individualistic attitude has become noticeable. Both single as well as married people may say that they have a right to a child, or at least a right to do what they want with their bodies i.e. donating sperm or ova or providing surrogate motherhood. The full consequences of such attitudes have yet to be seen but let it not be supposed that this will prove a minor factor in our national life. We are on a slippery slope and the failure of the Church of England uncompromisingly to uphold the sacramental character of marriage and hence the integrity of family life may well be a major factor in the decline of moral standards going far beyond the family itself.

If the Church is to say something authoritative about marriage and the family it will have to pay particular regard to parental roles. Let us briefly do this in the context of our discussion of artificial reproduction. To begin with we can fairly easily make the distinction between the biological relationship and the social relationship; the distinction made in latin between the *progenitor* and the *pater* and between the *progenetrix* and the *mater*. Mothers conceive and bear a child, fathers beget children. However, the most important role is that of the nurturing of the child, being parents in the social sense; the pater and mater.

Yet it may be argued that the social parentage does not just begin with the birth of a child, but with its conception, or perhaps more precisely when the couple decide to have a child or at latest discover one is on the way. At this point the father takes on a protective role and the mother an expectant one. They are collaborating in the creation of a child which when it is born they will both care for. This is the main reason why surrogate motherhood is unacceptable. The wife must bear the child. The question of sperm and oocyte is very much a secondary matter provided there is no secrecy about it. By secrecy we mean secrecy about the fact of artificial reproduction, not about the identity of donors. To be sure there is a long-standing acceptance of the view expressed by the report of the Board of Social Responsiblity in its evidence to the Inquiry into Human Fertilisation and Embryology, chaired by Dame Mary Warnock, which states that 'Anglican thought has had to consider its tradition that the unitive and procreative goods of marriage may not be separated.' Yet the Board acknowledges differences of opinion as to whether or not donated sperm or oocytes destroy the relationship between union and procreation. Already the strict view has been modified in the permission to use contraceptives. The Board emphasises, however, that marriage carries with it the promise and expectation of children. If the secrecy in artificial reproduction can be eliminated, even allowing for the anonymity of donors, so that the child has some knowledge of his genetic origin and the doctor keeps a genetic history of the donor, perhaps there is less objection to these artificial reproductive practices. After all we have said that what is most important is the integrity and welfare of the child. This aim is paramount in adoption where parents are screened very carefully. It should also be the case in other instances of family-making.

We may be urged to consider a balance of interests. Unlike adoption, where a child already exists and the task is to provide him with a good home, AID and donated oocytes are to create a child, and the need is not for a good home but to remedy a couple's childlessness; this is not to be child-centred. The motive is different from that of agencies placing a child for adoption. In artificial reproduction then there is even more reason for taking pains to ensure the child is well served. The parental role may normally be said to start with a decision and to progress through a pregnancy, and this is sound. Perhaps the genetic relationship, provided it is missing on one side only, may be regarded as of lesser importance. Can it be regulated to a minor position in the equation? It certainly cannot be ignored and, to pretend it is what it is not, is clearly indefensible. To allow some general knowledge of the donor, short of identification, may be thought to be the least that should be provided. Is it good enough for Christian people to think along these lines, or is it not better for the couple to come to terms with their childlessness? After all there is a distinct element of self-indulgence in AID and similar forms of artificial reproduction, and the faithful are not called to self-indulgence of their needs, especially those that are acquired needs, and it has to be said that the desire for children is largely a culturally acquired need.

The moral issues which face Christian people today need to be considered by the Church and by others as well. Indeed, the Church needs to consult widely in order properly to identify the issues and establish factual evidence. What it cannot do is to leave the decision to other people. There is a tendency to rely too much on the decisions of professional, administrative and political bodies. In the matter of artificial reproduction it would be a serious mistake to accept, without very careful thought, the decisions of professional medical organisations. They have to regulate the behaviour of their members, not all of whom are Christian, with a public in mind which reflects many and varied beliefs. Even the medical profession is divided on a number of matters. Indeed, in the matter of abortions the profession is polarised in almost two equal groups taking opposing views. There is some division of opinion about artificial reproduction.

However, we should observe carefully one aspect of modern medical practice that has developed in recent years. This is the marked tendency to extend treatment of diseases to include provision of services. Let us examine AID in this respect. Very generally AID is seen as a remedy for male infertility. It certainly cannot be regarded as treating a person, for the male is ignored. Rather it may be said to be treating the healthy wife for the infertility of her husband. This, however, is to stretch the word 'treatment'. What it is doing is remedying a couple's childlessness. In this it is usually willing to provide the service if it is within its competence to do so. Thus Sir John Peel's BMA Committee recommended it be provided by the National Health Service, which is now the case. In practice there is a marked tendency to provide it on demand. Thus it is known that both lesbian couples and single women have received AID. It is highly likely that before long transplanting embryos will not be uncommon. Organisations for providing surrogate mothers exist in the USA and one operates in the UK. The American College of Obstetricians and Gynaecologists last year issued some guidelines to its 24,000 members on their involvement with surrogate mothering. These guidelines recognise the current interest in the practice and make suggestions about medical collaboration in screening women and in the matters of their health care during pregnancy.

The conclusion seems inescapable that a medical profession will provide a service as well as treatment if there is a demand; if, that is to say, there is expression of a need either natural or acquired; and the profession will not do so only if there is legal prohibition or regulation, such as in the case of the use of dangerous drugs. A profession will minimally make value judgements about family life. This is because it takes a very individualistic view of its work. The doctor-patient relationship is central, confidential and individually orientated. Social considerations are not normally prominent unless public policy so decrees. This may be seen in the controversy about doctors providing contraceptive pills to girls under sixteen years of age without parental consent. For these reasons it is important that the Church should examine professional advice and practice critically and by no means devolve its responsibilities, even though many would define the problem as a medical one. In fact artificial reproduction using donated semen or oocytes is much more than a medical matter. This is so for both AID which is essentially a simple technique and does not require medical assistance and for IVF which is medically highly technical.

What is true of the professions is also true of the State. The government set up the Inquiry into Human Fertility and Embryology to discover what it must do by legislative or administrative means, and the Report is now being scrutinised. However, the state has to cope with a pluralistic society. It must set out minimum standards, not exemplary ones. The recommendations of the Warnock Inquiry are inevitably the result of compromises among its members, some medical others lay, some Christian others representing other religions and none; and on some matters they openly disagree in minority reports. Thus the faithful will inevitably turn to the Church not to the medical profession or the state for guidance.

When Keble preached he was very much aware of the role of the Church in the nation's affairs, hence his sermon on National Apostasy. Yet it is not necessarily the case today that the Church of England should pronounce on what everyone should believe and do, for we live in a country, unlike Keble, with Hindus, Jews, Muslims, Sikhs and unbelievers. What the Church may do, and it is surely agreed should do, is set the Christian standard. To be sure some of the faithful will fall short of it, possibly by no fault of their own, as in many broken marriages; but to declare what is desirable, to set the standard higher than what is required of all subjects of the realm may be to provide a light to guide us.

Certainly, let it not be said that the shepherds have neglected the sheep and allowed the flock to be scattered to become the prey of wolves. If this were so it would not be national apostasy but the apostasy of the national Church.

Duncan Mitchell is professor of sociology in the University of Exeter, and research fellow in the Institute of Population Studies, Exeter.

9
The mysterious leap of faith

Andrew Louth

Appeal to the Fathers has been a recurrent theme in the history of Anglican theology. So much so, that it has a fair claim to be one of its most distinctive features. The Reformers appealed to the Fathers against the corruptions of medieval Catholicism. Certainly, their appeal to the Fathers was somewhat haphazard — there were few reliable editions of the Fathers available — and was not distinctive of the English reformers as against the continentals. (Calvin too makes much of the Fathers). Nevertheless it was significant in the light of what was to come that Cranmer discussed Nazianzen and Chrysostom in his preface to the Great Bible, thus claiming that the 'open bible' is part of the tradition with patristic sanction, and drew on Greek liturgies (not that they are any more patristic than the Latin, however) in the compilation of the *Book of Common Prayer*.

But when we come to Richard Hooker, and the great flowering of Anglican theology that followed in the wake of the *Ecclesiastical Polity* — the Caroline Divines, whose acme was the sermons and prayers of Lancelot Andrewes — here we find a veritable tapestry of patristic recollection. The writings of Jeremy Taylor, Bramhall and others expanded into a tradition that revived again after the Civil War in such as John Pearson and Bishop Bull, and reflected the profound and far-reaching influence of the Fathers — especially perhaps the Greek Fathers. But the impact of the Fathers continues beyond that classic period. It is important for the Cambridge Platonists. Cudworth in particular was deeply learned in the Greek Fathers and influenced by them. There are echoes of the Fathers in England even in the *grand siecle* of the Enlightenment, the eighteenth century: Berkeley and Butler were influenced by Origen. And with the Oxford Movement, it hardly needs to be said how important the Fathers were.

One of the great publishing feats of the Oxford Movement — along with the *Tracts for the Times* and the *Library of Anglo-Catholic Theology* —

was the publication of the *Library of the Fathers*, begun by Newman and Pusey in the 1830s and continued by Pusey almost up to his death, which made the Fathers available to the English reader as never before (it forms the basis of the *Ante-Nicene Christian Library* and the *Library of Nicene and Post-Nicene Fathers* which are still the standard English translation of the patristic writings.) For Newman especially the question of the renewal of the Church was simply an attempt to discover the Church of the Fathers, and when he found it in the Church in communion with the Roman See, his fate was settled.

But it was not only the Oxford Movement within nineteenth century Anglicanism that looked back to the Fathers: the very different Anglicanism, scholarly, liberal, deeply concerned with social issues, associated with the names of the three great Cambridge scholars, Westcott, Lightfoot and Hort, also experienced the quickening influence of the Fathers — again, especially the Greek Fathers. Hort in particular drew heavily on their inspiration in his profound reflections on Christian discipleship found in his Hulsean Lectures, *The Way the Truth the Life*. And one could easily point to others since their day within the Anglican fold who have drawn on the inspiration of the Fathers.

Such a survey, for all its gaps, reveals one thing at least: that it would be wrong to associate an appeal to the Fathers with any kind of dead antiquarianism. What we have above is practically a roll call of all the creative periods of Anglican theology. The Fathers have not been simply appealed to as some kind of brake on too great an indulgence in speculative flights of theology; more often indeed it might seem that they provided launching pads for such speculative flights. Cudworth was no hide-bound conservative, nor was Westcott. Rather it would seem that the Fathers have opened the doors to a vision of much greater depth and power than one might have expected in the centuries between the Reformation and now. Any tendency to reduce theology simply to human reflection on the religious possibilities of human experience has received a jolt from the patristic vision. The proper study of mankind is *not* man: for man is created in the image of God, called to know and love God, called to share with God in a task of cosmic dimensions: the restoration of a world that has fallen out with itself, because it has fallen out with God.

But what *kind* of inspiration has Anglican theology found in the Fathers, and has that inspiration any power today, or has it run out? The influence of the Fathers on the Oxford Movement, the most important development in English religion since the Reformation, reveals an influence far from narrowly academic.

In the 1830s — the really creative decade for the Oxford Movement when Keble, Pusey and Newman all found themselves possessed by a vision and enthusiasm as perhaps at no other time — Pusey gave a course of lectures on 'Types and Prophecies of the Old Testament'.[1] That looks on the face of it a normal and dull enough occupation for the Regius Professor of Hebrew in the University of Oxford. But in these lectures Pusey tries to expound and understand the way of interpreting Scripture characteristic of the Fathers, the way of allegory or typology (Pusey's word, and maybe his coinage: OED records no earlier instance). And that is something different, for Pusey had no illusions about the magnitude of the task he was undertaking. Like Keble in his later Tract LXXXIX, 'On the Mysticism attributed to the Early Fathers of the Church', Pusey saw the patristic use of allegory as that aspect of patristic theology most remote from, and most distasteful to, the intellectual climate of his day. In attempting to enter into the Fathers' use of allegory with understanding and appreciation, Pusey knows that he is challenging the whole approach in matters of religion and theology characteristic of his contemporaries, and so he lays his foundations broad and deep. It is not simply a matter of defending a quaint style of interpretation (or one that *seems* quaint), it is a matter of questioning fundamental assumptions and trying to replace them. So the early pages of these lectures are concerned with the question as to how we reach conclusions in matters of religion, what evidence counts, how we are to argue — or rather, Pusey tries to show that a concern with evidence, narrowly conceived, and argument, as the exercise of man's ratiocinative faculty, themselves undermine the way by which in religious matters we come to the truth. Pusey says:

> Our conviction also is of a compound character and made up of various emotions: in moral subjects it cannot be mainly intellectual: in Divine things, awe, wonder, an absorbing sense of infinity, or of purity, or of holiness infuse conviction more directly than reasoning; nay, reasoning, in that it appeals to one faculty only, and that for the time is erected into a judge, and so, as it were, sits superior, constantly goes directly counter to the frame of mind, wherein belief is received. The chance sight (so to say) of a flower illuminated by the sun's rays, or of the starry heavens, 'the moon and the stars which God has ordained', impress the feeling of God upon the soul more than any artificial reasoning from final causes. Like the centurion by the cross we are awed into belief. God also has so constituted us, that impression is most strongly made upon us *incidentally*. (P6)

From this it is quite clear that Pusey saw the main problem that

1. Unpublished. The MS is in Pusey House Library, Oxford. References in text: P + leaf number.

separated his age from the thought-world of the Fathers (and, correspondingly, the main contribution the Fathers had to make to the task of theology in his day) to lie in the way modern man had tended to constrict the focus of his approach to reality to the *reason*, narrowly conceived as a discursive, argumentative faculty. It is by arguing from evidence along the regular paths of reason that man arrives at the truth: other ways of attaining to the truth — through our feelings and emotions, through trust in others — are dismissed. So Pusey had earlier said, 'This is the case with regard to our whole creed; by striving overmuch at clearness, and practically admitting only what they could make, as they thought, intelligible to themselves, men have narrowed it far below that of the ancient Church or of our own in former days' (P3).

Modern man limits reality to what he can render intelligible, and naturally enough in this realm he can make progress only as science advances. But it is utterly anthropocentric to limit reality to what man can render intelligible to himself, even if much of what can be rendered thus intelligible seems strange and exciting. Man has advanced in his understanding of the structure of the atom because what cannot be measured and rendered intelligible in that way can (it seems) be safely ignored. We do much less well in understanding elections because what cannot be measured there — the curious ways in which human beings behave — is actually determinative.

For the Fathers the symbol of man's mysteriousness, which prevents him from being finally dissected by reason, is the doctrine of man created in the image of God. The ultimate mysteriousness of the unknowable God is reflected in His image, man, and so the personal is seen as something we cannot ultimately dominate or control. But that fundamental mysteriousness of man is, in some way, ordered towards God the creator, and so Pusey sees belief as a kind of primordial acknowledgement of God, prescinding from reasoning processes, much more responsive to the allure of purity or holiness or beauty or mystery than to the narrower grounds we call evidence: 'Belief also (not *conviction* produced by argument whereby a man is as the word expresses "convicted" rather than led to believe — but unreasoning belief) is, as well as unbelief, deeply rooted in the human mind; and whenever witnessed it appeals to an original principle of our nature, which — because pure and from God, and [since it is] a relic of our uncorrupted nature, and a consequence of our original derivation from the breath of God, so that we recognise our Father's and Maker's voice — has a mysterious, talismanic control over our souls' (P14-15).

Pusey then draws from the Fathers a sense of the mysteriousness of

God which is echoed in the mysteriousness of man, His image, in the mystery of the personal. Because of this he resists any attempt to reduce the parameters of the world to reason, which is only a part of man, and which only discloses to man a part of the world, only a part of himself, and very little of any significance about God at all. 'Awe, wonder, an absorbing sense of infinity, or of purity, or of holiness': these are much surer guides in matters that touch on the ultimate mysteries of life and being.

This sense of *mystery* stands at the heart of the legacy of the Fathers as Pusey and the other Tractarians perceived it: a mystery that calls forth awe and humility from man, but at the same time lends to man a much greater dignity as the image of God Himself than he can appreciate if he arrogates to himself a position of dominance through reliance on calculative reason. But it is a mystery that finds historical lineaments in the Incarnate Word, Jesus Christ: it is not a vague sense of mysteriousness that makes no demands on the individual but leaves him in comfortable vagueness.

Newman too spoke of this sense of mystery and the ultimate indefinability of divine truth: '. . . freedom from symbols and articles is abstractedly the highest state of Christian communion, and the peculiar privilege of the primitive Church . . . because when confessions do not exist, the mysteries of divine truth, instead of being exposed to the gaze of the profane and uninstructed, are kept hidden in the bosom of the Church, far more faithfully than is otherwise possible . . .'[2] But, he said, his avowal of this was 'not from any tenderness towards that proud impatience of control in which many exult': for it is part of the lesson of the Fathers that the mystery of God in Jesus Christ is not dissolved, but kept more firmly in focus, when it is professed in creeds and conciliar definitions.

This combination of a sense of ultimate unfathomable mystery with the insistence that the approach to this mystery and even its lineaments, to some extent, can be definitely defined, is ultimately rooted in the heart of the Christian creed: that the mystery of God is manifest in the person of Jesus of Nazareth. The heresies that the Fathers faced and rejected — and for whose rejecting they developed creeds and definitions — can be seen as attempts to dissolve the mystery, or to blur its focus in the person of our Lord. Gnosticism dissolves the mystery of God altogether by turning it into a cosmic projection of human anxiety; Arianism and docetism in quite different ways break the link between

2. *Arians of the Fourth Century* (London, 4th edn. 1876), pp.36-7.

the mystery of God and the person of Christ; Apollinarianism does not allow the mystery of God to bear upon the *whole* human condition; Nestorianism merely juxtaposes the mystery of God and the person of Christ. The Christological definitions, then, safeguard the indissoluble connection between the mystery of God and the person of Christ; the doctrine of the Trinity provides a context that makes that connection intelligible — for reason is not denied in our experience of God, though reason alone cannot effect for us that experience.

A combination of unfathomable mystery and definite historical fact: it is a combination that meets us at every turn in the texture of Catholic Christianity — and it is a combination that is very uncomfortable for the masterful ratiocinative faculty, which, in our culture, has become accustomed to the role of supreme arbiter. Indeed it is not just the combination that is uncomfortable: it is each element thus combined taken on its own.

Unfathomable mystery is obviously unacceptable: mysteries are merely problems for the discursive reason, to be tackled, resolved and disposed of. A mystery that remains mysterious and unfathomable even as it discloses itself: that is too bewildering for the understanding — even though in every real encounter between persons we find something analogous to just such a mystery. For if in our encounter with others we come to understand them, control and dominate them, and are not content to allow them their freedom in which they ultimately escape our understanding and control, then we have ceased to treat them as *persons*. In dominating them we depersonalize them, and ourselves. As Simone Weil put it, might's 'power to transform a man into a thing is double and it cuts both ways; it petrifies differently but equally the souls of those who suffer it, and of those who wield it.'[3]

But the definite historical fact — whether the historical reality of our Incarnate Lord, or the historical structure of the Church (which reason tells us is contingent and might thus have been otherwise), or the particular events through which the divine will calls out to us — such definite historical fact is equally unacceptable to reason. 'Accidental truths of history can never become the proof of necessary truths of reason': Lessing's dictum exactly expresses rationalism's unease with the historical. The historical might have been otherwise, it is arbitrary: let *us* then fashion things as we please.

And so everything borne to us by the tradition of the Church — the Scriptures (an *arbitrary* collection of Israelite and early Christian

3. *Intimations of Christianity among the Ancient Greeks* (London 1957), pp. 44-5.

literature: for the canon is contingent and might have been otherwise), the three-fold apostolic ministry (an historical accident), creeds, councils and definitions (culturally and politically determined) — is relativised. The faith then becomes something *we* fashion on the basis of the evidence (alas mediated by tradition, but that can't be helped) as it appears to us. It is changed from being something we receive from the past, from those whom we can recognize as Fathers, to whom we have the humility to listen and from whom we hope to learn. Of course there is the task of attempting to distinguish between Tradition and traditions: but the recognition of the validity of such a task should not lead us to 'narrow our gaze' to what can be rendered clear and intelligible, and thus cease to listen to Tradition in the expectation of hearing there the Voice of the Shepherd speaking from the depths of the experience of the Church and calling to us as His own.

So Hort (whom no-one could regard as an anti-intellectual antiquarian) could say, 'The history of the Church from its foundation to the present day is hardly less necessary to the Church at large than the Gospel itself, whatever it may be to the individual disciple . . . "Have I been so long time with you and yet hast thou not known me?" Such is the language in which we may still hear our Lord recalling us to an undervalued and imperfectly used experience.'[4]

There are two further implications of hearing the patristic challenge that Pusey draws out. Both of them can be seen as consequences of the attempt to transcend a merely intellectual rationalism: first, there is a refusal to overconceptualize theology; secondly, an awareness of the role of the body and the senses in our response to God.

So Pusey speaks of the modern 'attempt to substitute abstract, and as they would fain have it, clearer terms for the types and typical language' of the Bible, in which 'they uniformly by this transmutation evaporate much of their meaning' (P24). Rather theology should dwell on these types and symbols, and in this way it comes to draw closer to poetry: an analogy Pusey notices, and Keble draws out in his Tract LXXXIX:

> Poetry, traced as high up as we can go, may almost seem to be God's gift from the beginning, vouchsafed to us for this very purpose [viz., to be 'the channel of supernatural knowledge to mankind'] . . . And since the characteristic tendency of poetical minds is to make the world of sense, from beginning to end, symbolical of the absent and unseen, any instance of divine favour shown to Poetry, any divine use of it in the training of God's people, would seem, as far as it goes, to warrant that tendency; to set God's seal upon it, and witness it as reasonable and true.[5]

4. *The Way the Truth the Life* (London, 1897 edn.), p.35.
5. *On the Mysticism attributed to the Early Fathers of the Church* (London, 2nd edn. 1868), pp. 189-90.

But we should note that this analogy between theology and poetry is not intended to suggest that theology is a vague subject appealing to the emotions rather than the intellect (as some modern liberal theologians seem to suggest — cf. *The Myth of God Incarnate*), rather theology as analogous to the poetical is a more exacting discipline than a merely conceptualized theology could ever be, attempting a closer and more precise attention to the lineaments of God's revelation in the tapestry of type and symbol, whose pattern is discerned in the light of Incarnation. More exacting: for such a theology requires of us a deeper sensitivity and deprives us of the crutch of reliance on procedure provided by a merely rational theology. It is more alarming, more dangerous: but more real.

But secondly, in avoiding a mere intellectualism, we begin to rediscover the role of the body and senses in our knowledge of God — or better engagement with God (unless we are sure we hear the biblical echoes of the word 'knowledge'). It is often thought that the Fathers had little place for the body and the senses, being 'ascetic' and 'Platonic'. It is certainly true that much in their intellectual atmosphere militated against any positive appreciation of the body, but then their holding to the doctrine of the resurrection of the body,their attachment to a rich sacramental theology, and the development of Christian art and poetry become even more noteworthy. 'The glory of God is a living man, and the life of man is the vision of God'[6]: that phrase of Irenaeus's sums up the patristic understanding of the role of the *whole* man in his encounter with God. Seen in this light, it is not surprising that Tractarianism led to 'ritualism' and a largely successful attempt to save the Church of England from a pattern of worship that had degenerated into continual relays of information, or mere expressions of emotion. How far that has been frittered away in the cerebral and often, it seems, deliberately ugly concoctions of recent liturgical reform is a matter for regret and heart-searching. But the drawing of the senses into our engagement with God means a renewed sympathy with the sacramental vision of the Fathers. Their sacramentalism did not shrink from drawing on frankly aesthetic categories to make the symbolic structure of the liturgy subserve that sense of the Church in the liturgy as standing on the threshold of the world to come. It is a sense that the Orthodox Church's liturgy has never lost.

As the conceptual simply seeks clarity and sees truth in terms of exact correspondence, so an engagement that involves the senses is less patient of mere clarity and sees the truth in terms of sympathy. And as Hort remarked, 'aesthetic perception is part of sympathy. The highest art is that which most weaves together sympathies of various orders, i.e. is in the truest sense sacramental.'[6] Only by rediscovering that kind of sacramentality will the Church of today be able to present a vision of the glory of God revealed in her crucified Lord that will speak compellingly to our world. And for that task the appeal to the Fathers is as relevant as ever.

Andrew Louth was formerly chaplain of Worcester College, Oxford.

6. Op. cit. (n. 4), p. 174.

10
New annunciations

Tom Sutcliffe

The free-standing altar, the priest facing the people across it, this new, by now almost universal arrangement for the liturgy of the eucharist is more than cosmetic. It tellingly symbolises the spirit of the Second Vatican Council. The reaction of the church to Enlightenment and the industrial and scientific revolutions of the nineteenth century was initially to withdraw within itself. The First Vatican Council was egocentric and obsessive. But now, stirred by the therapy and analysis prescribed by Pope John XXIII and applied by Pope Paul VI, the church faces the world.

Moreover the church learns from the world. It no longer deplores modern life as probably evil. In *Pacem in Terris*, the monumental and humane encyclical that is Pope John's testament, the church embraces sociological and political progress. Conditions are better for the working classes. Women are taking a fuller, more active part in political life. Finally, 'imperialism is rapidly becoming an anachronism'. The debate on how the church should relate to the world continues. Cardinal Ratzinger has criticised aspects of Liberation Theology, reminding of 'the universality of the law of fraternal love,' and warning against 'the politicisation of existence which, misunderstanding the entire meaning of the Kingdom of God and the transcendence of the person, begins to sacralise politics and betray the religion of the people in favour of the projects of the revolution.' Pope John-Paul II appears to want to endorse the Anglican situation in England, where clergy are debarred by law from taking an active part in politics along with lunatics and peers of the realm. Yet in Canada he denounced companies that are 'exposed to the temptation of responding only to the marketplace,' and called for 'collective agreements between workers and management and some forms of joint ownership.' The 'option for the poor', pioneered by the Anglican Tractarians in the nineteenth century but increasingly neglected by Anglicans during the last fifty years, is now official Vatican policy. The bourgeois revolutions against which Pio Nono fulminated are fully exonerated by the church: how long before Mao and Lenin are reinterpreted and absorbed by the inexorable progress of Vatican exegetics?

Just as the church has struggled with the problem of deciding what can be regarded as a 'just' war, so it is now debating what is a 'just' society, and whether an unjust social system can be opposed in good conscience even to the extent of violent revolution. The church believes in human rights. It is extraordinary that the Bishop of Durham's intervention in the coal dispute, with its eye-catching if uncharitable phrase about an 'elderly, imported American', could have led some people to question whether Anglican bishops should engage in political debate. Bishops and clergy, on the contrary, cannot in conscience remain silent about political and economic injustice, where they perceive it — though they must expect economic diagnosis to be met by economic rebuttal, and social prescriptions to be democratically discussed. The Anglican church is proud to include in its tradition the intervention of Bishop Wilberforce in the cause of emancipation and the abolition of the slave trade. It is proud to have among its bishops Trevor Huddleston, author of *Naught for Your Comfort*, a denunciation of racial injustice in South Africa that helped to turn that unhappy country out of the British Commonwealth of Nations.

But if the church engages critically with the world in order more effectively to fulfil its mission, it may also need to adapt its own order and formation to serve that purpose. 'The past will never return,' wrote Angelo Roncalli in 1933. 'New situations require new dispositions.' It is impossible to read Peter Hebblethwaite's definitive biography of Pope John* without warming to Roncalli's positive optimism and sharing his recognition of the necessity to be open to change. Naturally Pope John did not seek change in the church for its own sake, and strongly opposed, for instance, the relaxation of the rule of priestly celibacy. But he recognised the Holy Spirit at work in many of the changes affecting the world around him. The papal smile, the sense of love for creation, replaced the monitory papal finger. When Pope John addressed the opening session of his great ecumenical council, with its appeal beyond the bounds of catholicity to the entire range of christian believers and even unbelievers, he said, 'Today Providence is guiding us towards a new order of human relationships which, thanks to human efforts and

---

**John XXIII Pope of the Council* (Geoffrey Chapman, 1984).

yet far surpassing its hopes, will bring us to the realisation of still higher and undreamed of expectations.' These words were being used within a few days of the eruption of the Cuban missile crisis, but John's faith in the goodness of creation never wavered.

The Vatican Council, Pope John suggested, would be expected to provide a leap forward in doctrinal insight. But 'authentic doctrine has to be studied and expounded in the light of the research methods and the language of modern thought. . . . For the substance of the ancient deposit of faith is one thing, and the way in which it is presented is another.'

Today the church endorses the dignity of individual human rights, the idea of democracy, of freedom of religion. It sets itself against the exploitation of poverty. It proclaims the equality of women and men not just *sub specie aeternitatis* but in this life. The 'civilisation of love' about which Pope John Paul talks, the recognition of universal community, such notions may be utopian but they are guiding principles. And they provide the proper context for the most pressing controversy in the Church of England — the debate about the ordination of women to the priesthood.

There have been many papers and books arguing both sides of the case. Sara Maitland in *A map of the new Country** adopts a refreshingly open, almost non-committal approach. But it is hard to remain untouched by the witness that her book represents. Renewal has to be a constant Christian theme. Christianity in the 1980s *is* a new country. Yet the most attractive virtue of Sara Maitland's examination of women and Christianity is that it is rooted in a profoundly orthodox sense of what is Christian. It is not a clarion call to sudden revolution, but a careful enquiry into all sorts of assumptions and the theology that accompanies them.

This new country is a Christian world in which many women share a sense of systematic exclusion from power and responsibility within the context of their belief. And they are doing something about it. Opponents of women's ordination to the priesthood are inclined to dismiss the well-attested opinion of the public on the matter as simply untutored. But perhaps the people are wiser than they are given credit for being. The ultimate authentication of theology and of church order depends on acceptance by the people of God. The sacred ministry springs from the people with the inspiration of God. It is a factor to be

---

**A map of the new Country – Women and Christianity* (Routledge and Kegan Paul, 1983)

taken into account if the great generality of people consider women to be eligible for the priesthood, as they do. Especially during the reign of a Queen and the government of a female Prime Minister, the marshalling of arguments against women's ordination can seem wilfully negativistic.

Inevitably, Sara Maitland's readers anticipate a full frontal rehearsal of the familiar arguments in favour of women's ordination, and of course she does include a chapter on the subject. But it is handled in a restrained theological sense. There is no hysterical assertion of presumed rights, but instead an opening up of the entire question of priesthood.

Sara is the wife of an Anglican priest, and a mother of two. She is anxious that if women are ordained priest it does not reinforce the misguided but widespread opinion that priests are a superior breed of Christian. She appreciates the potential of the ordered church as an effective agent of mission, but she continually returns to the object which mission should pursue. Orthodoxy is usually identified with received positions, the sense of everything cut and dried. The orthodox Christian life, she observes, is a journey through a new country, a country made new by the Christian understanding. In that state of perpetual pilgrimage the traveller needs such a map as she provides.

Because her book is primarily addressed to women, it is healthily disorientating for men. Most books, from their language, seem to assume a masculine readership as the norm. When, as here, the method is the reverse the male reader's initial reaction may well be irritation. But there can be a therapeutic effect. The male reader can come to see that it is indeed a new country where Christian women need to communicate a specifically women's perspective about their work within Christianity. The very method of writing is a lesson for men in the dislocation between women and Christianity. All readers will be able to draw useful analogies about the denial of Christ in the wilful subjugation of one human being by another.

The male reader may bridle at some of the arguments, parading details of accidental and intentional sexism. Perhaps insufficient account is taken of some elements basic to traditional Christianity. Feminist suspicions about the earliest phase of the religion have to be set against the outcome of the early controversy over the Mosaic laws. Then, the masculine initiation rite of circumcision was replaced by the universal initiation rite of baptism, and baptised men and women were equally Christian. The reservation of the ordained ministries to men, following Jesus's calling of male apostles, should not be taken as a rejection of the spiritual potential of women in the light of the appearance of the resurrected Jesus to women as his first witnesses. At that time women would have been completely unacceptable as witnesses in any Jewish court, so the choice of women witnesses is significant. Yet for church order to have been dominated by men for almost 2000 years may suggest that there is more to the specialisation than built-in misogynism (which was the secret attraction, after all, of mithraism). If Christianity had not articulated a sensible view at the time of the relationship between the genders, could it have gained such wide acceptance?

There is a big problem, though. As Sara writes in her chapter on 'Roots and beginnings', 'Once the divine is securely identified as male, however subconsciously, women become less divine than men; and for Christianity that also meant less human. Whether they are despised as "carnal" or exalted as "inspiring" they no longer have to be treated as though they were fully human people, made in the image of God.' There may be nothing unconscious about the identification of the divine with masculine humanity, in the second person of the Trinity, god and man-in-both-senses, that essential fact of incarnation. But Sara insists that, though the masculinity of Jesus is a necessary accident of his perfect humanity, it must not mask the sense of God as capable of both modes of sexuality. Choosing to become *man* does not imply deficiency in women, any more than the example of the Virgin Mary ('Fiat mihi') implies that men are less apt to conform with the divine pattern.

The trouble is that, when we consider the historic, anthropological reality of God in the Jewish as well as the Christian past, the patriarchal dimension inevitably assumes a kind of consequence. Against which must be balanced Paul's words to the Galatians: 'As many of you as have been baptised into Christ have put on Christ. There is neither Jew nor Greek, there is neither bond nor free, there is neither male nor female: for ye are all one in Christ Jesus.' It must be wrong to see God as limited to the male aspect, which is a likely result of the male-only priesthood.

The equations of theology, as of algebra, can be applied in various ways. How the results add up reflects the earthly circumstances of the believer in question, who does not exist in a celestial vacuum. The church will have to accomodate women's changed perception of their role in the world. It has approved the change, but not yet pursued the logic of it into its own structures.

Sara Maitland believes that women have a special duty in today's church to carry out a prophetic role, as they had in the church of Paul's day. Women may explain the obligations of Christianity all the more effectively precisely because they have so long been excluded from church order. To judge from the flagging evangelisation of modern

European society under the existing, male-dominated church order, all sorts of new ministries, including the ministry of women in the priesthood, may be needed. Male readers may find this claim presumptuous. But nobody can deny that women in church circles are still as they have long been excluded from equivalent authority as members of Christ.

In Sara's case, the road to Damascus went through American feminism. She saw the received orthodoxies differently as a result of her direct experience of the Women's Movement in the US, and also recognised the results it had achieved on behalf of women. Communities of nuns, the most obvious manifestation of exclusive female Christianity, had also she observed come to recognise the problem that exists between women and Christianity. And in the church bureaucracies, on the other hand, women's role is commanding if rarely noticed. Administration would founder without women.

On the other hand she is comparatively unconcerned about the implicit sexism in the language of the liturgies and bible, and happy to continue with the generalised use of the male gender in collective instances. And she certainly rejects that aspect of the movement for the ordination of women, among some women theologians in the US, which regards women priests almost as the necessary preliminary to the abolition of the priesthood as such. Clearly if women are ordained priest in the Church of England, it will be vital to avoid the sense of wounded dignity that the controversies about women's ordination have given many American women priests, as a result of which too few have achieved parish priest status. Too many of the proponents of women's ordination are inspired by a conviction of personal vocation and are reluctant to test that vocation through the normal processes of the church. The risk is that if all these subjective vocations were to be too rashly entertained, it would simply enhance clerical dominance and the sense of the priesthood as superior, rather than a service to all.

Yet there is still something almost too Utopian in Sara's image of her new Jerusalem. The new spirituality which she proclaims, and which she sees women representing, is almost as demanding as it was in the desert days of St Anthony.

The question of women and the church is above all a question of community. Christianity is not just a religion about God, not just a matter of thanksgiving and repentance, of fear of divine retribution and loathing of the corrupt, lapsed stuff of human existence. Christianity is a religion about humanity: we are in principle committed to community with every other human being, whether the others believe in God or not. That is the answer to those who, seeing the secularity of modern life in

Britain and elsewhere, want Christians to become ever more exclusive brethren. The need to face life expressed by Pope John was also asserted by Mother Julian of Norwich.

When Christians contemplate the divine, they see God's grace poured out continuously in the person of Jesus, man and God, redeemer of all. Beyond God, Christians see their fellow human beings, challenging their fellowship precisely as God was challenged by his lapsed creation, the need he answered by becoming human. If God is our fellow, how can we deny community to any human? This is the vital claim and obligation of Christians. We do not tolerate the evaluation of human living as worthwhile or not worthwhile, that evaluation implicit in euthanasia and casual abortion. Life is always worth living, since every living soul is capable of love and community.

Christians cannot be open to the divine grace on which they depend, if they do not strive for the community of all. Whatever fractures that community must concern all Christians. When the whole community was automatically Christian, the particular sexual identifications at the centre of church order were unremarked. But nowadays there is a profound sense of dislocation at the heart of Christianity experienced by many women, and it demands urgent remedy. The plea to reform the priesthood needs to be answered.

Tom Sutcliffe is a journalist on the Guardian.

St Mary the Virgin
Bourne Street, Pimlico, London SW1

The Clergy

Father John Gilling/parish priest, Father Timothy Bugby/assistant priest, Dr E. L. Mascall, OGS/honorary assistant priest, Dr Brian Horne/honorary assistant priest.

Services (subject to alteration)

Sundays — Low Mass 0800 and 1900, Parish Mass with hymns 0945, High Mass and sermon 1100, Evensong 1815, Solemn Benediction 1830.
Weekdays — Mass: Monday, Tuesday, Thursday 0730 and 1830, Wednesday 1130 and 1830, Friday 0730 and 1130, Saturday 0800 and 1130.
Evensong: 1800 (daily). Benediction: Saturday 1815.

How to get to St Mary's

From Sloane Square underground station turn left along Holbein Place; first left at Whittaker Street; turn right into Bourne Street and the church is on the left. Total distance: 200 metres. Buses to Sloane Square: 11, 19, 22, 137. For information about house groups, prayer groups and instruction, contact one of the staff at St Mary's Presbytery, 30 Bourne Street, London SW1W 8JJ. Telephone: 01-730 2423.